CHRISTMAS
Treasures

Over 50 Gifts, Ornaments, and Decorations
to Craft and Stitch

By Robby Smith

Photographs by Jon Aron

Meredith® Press
New York, New York

Credits

Photography: *Jon Aron*
Stylist: *Leslie Linsley*
Illustrations: *Greg Worth*
Crafters: *Corrinne Allesandrello, Helen Jenkins,*
Else Knudson, Anne Lane, Ruth Linsley,
Gita Lundgren, Suzi Peterson, Liz Putur,
and *Mary Smith*

For Meredith® Press:

Director: *Elizabeth P. Rice*
Editorial Project Manager: *Barbara S. Machtiger*
Project Editor: *Sydne Matus*
Editorial Assistant: *Valerie Martone*
Production Manager: *Bill Rose*
Designer: *Diane Wagner*
Cover Photography: *Robert Gattullo*

Dear Reader:

Before you know it, Christmas will be here again, so now is the time to be thinking about the holiday decorations you'd like to deck your halls—and walls, windows, doors, gifts, and tree—with this festive season.

Let Robby Smith's *Christmas Treasures* make it easy for you. Here is an exciting and imaginative collection of more than fifty gifts, decorations, and ornaments you can create for yourself, your home, family and friends, and as stocking stuffers and bazaar items.

Begin with common, inexpensive materials and a minimum of skill, then follow the simple step-by-step instructions to quilt, appliqué, cross-stitch, crochet, cut, sew, and paste a treasure-trove of Christmas goodies in no time.

Meredith® Press is proud of *Christmas Treasures,* as we are of all the high-quality craft books we publish. Our commitment is to give our readers books with a variety of projects for every skill level; accurate, easy-to-follow instructions; full-color photographs; and clear diagrams and patterns—full size, whenever possible.

Wishing you the pleasures of holiday crafting.

Sincerely,

Barbara Machtiger

Editorial Project Manager
Meredith® Press

Contents

Introduction

Christmastime brings out the creativeness in all of us. It's so much fun to make things to give as gifts, for decorating our homes and trees, and to sell at holiday bazaars. When you make things for Christmas, the season becomes more exciting. The anticipation of giving and decorating with handmade projects creates an aura throughout the house.

The thing that I like best about crafting at Christmastime is that the stores are filled with materials that one doesn't always find at other times of the year. The manufacturers seem to bring out new products that make it easier to do whatever was difficult before. And the fabric shops are filled with all sorts of wonderful fabrics and trimmings.

Once everything is made, the fun of decorating is enjoyed by all. This year we added many handmade ornaments and decorations to those we made last year and the year before. Every year the tree gets more elaborate and different styles are added, depending on current trends. I think you'll find a wide variety of designs and projects to choose from.

All patterns are provided full size for every project in the book. We've tried to be responsive to the general complaint among crafters about enlarging patterns. Simply stated, nobody wants to enlarge a pattern if it is possible not to. We've been working on this in the studio. Every time we come up with an idea we try to see how it can be designed so the full-size pattern will fit on a book page. After that, we work on perfecting the directions. We're always looking for shortcuts and ways to do things better without sacrificing the design. It's an exciting challenge and I think you'll like the results.

—R. S.

Crafting How-To's and Materials

Throughout the book you will find a variety of projects to make using different crafting techniques. Most are simple sewing projects. While each project features specific step-by-step directions, there are some general tips and how-to's that pertain to all the projects. These can be most helpful, especially when you are working on several items at once.

When making Christmas ornaments, for example, you may find it cost- and time-efficient to make more than one at a time. A few tips for shortcuts and suggestions for materials will be helpful. In addition, we've discovered that there are always new and improved products on the market to ease the crafting process. Those that we've tested in our studio and found worthy of recommendation are suggested. Sometimes a specific brand of product is better than another and we like to mention this.

The following information and general directions will tell you the best ways to do various steps for several projects throughout the book. They'll also help you prepare the materials needed in the most efficient way. Further, there are suggestions for making things in quantity. This is especially useful if you are planning a Christmas bazaar.

FABRICS

Most fabrics come 45 inches wide and we try to design everything in the studio to take advantage of this in order to get the most efficient and economical use of fabric. When the pattern measurements for a project are dependent on using 45-inch-wide fabric, it is stated at the beginning of the materials list. If it is not mentioned, this means that any width is acceptable because the 45-inch width of the fabric is not needed to cut any pattern piece. For example, if you are making a wallhanging that is 44 inches wide, you could not use a background fabric that is 36 inches wide without piecing it, which would be unattractive.

Felt: Almost any fabric can be used for making Christmas ornaments, stockings, gifts, and home decorations. However, felt is one of the best materials for Christmas projects and works well for many reasons: It won't fray and therefore doesn't have to be hemmed, it comes in a wide range of colors, it's easy to glue pieces together in order to create an elaborate appliqué, and you can buy it in pieces as small as 9 × 12 inches or by the yard. Often felt can be found in wider widths than other material, which makes it especially good for creating a tablecover, banner, or tree skirt, for example.

Some felt is made with a fusible backing. Once a pattern piece is cut out it can be fused to another piece of fabric with a hot iron. This is an excellent product, but the colors are limited and it is not always available.

However, any fabric can be made fusible with fusible webbing, such as Stitch Witchery™, and a product called Transfuse II™, both by Stacy and available in most fabric and craft stores. These are products we use all the time and recommend when layers of fabric pieces are needed to make an appliqué, or when details are added to projects that are made in quantity, such as ornaments. This is a cleaner and easier method than gluing. Transfuse II looks like a sheet of thin plastic and is used to prepare the fabric *before* cutting the pattern pieces. And this is its main attraction! Here's how it works:

1. Place the fusible webbing on the back of any fabric.
2. Then place the Transfuse II on top of it and press with a medium hot iron as directed on the package.
3. Peel away the Transfuse II and the back of the fabric is fusible. You can now cut all pattern pieces, no matter how small, from the fabric and fuse to another piece of fabric without gluing or inserting another layer of fusible webbing. This makes it extremely easy to cut felt ornaments and all the little details that make up a design.

Other Fabrics: Muslin is a good, inexpensive material for backing pillows and stockings and some stuffed ornaments. Muslin can be found 36, 45, and sometimes 52 and 60 inches wide, which makes it excellent to use as a quilt backing. Small overall prints like calico are good choices for small projects as well as for quilts and pillows.

Even-weave for counted cross-stitch: Aida is the most commonly used fabric for counted cross-stitch. This fabric looks like linen and comes 18, 14, and 11 squares to the inch. We've used 14 count exclusively for the projects here. Aida cloth is most commonly sold in 12 × 18-inch pieces. It is 100 percent cotton and therefore washable. It comes in many colors, including white and ecru.

The pillows on page 42 were made with a product called Hopscotch by Charles Craft. This is a piece of even-weave fabric that comes in standard pillow sizes, and the plain center square provided for the cross-stitching is surrounded by a border of color. All materials for cross-stitch are available in craft stores.

STUFFING

Poly-Fil™ stuffing from Fairfield Processing Corporation was used to stuff all the ornaments, pillows, and small projects. Other manufacturers make stuffing, but this company's products seem to be most readily available in fabric stores and five-and-tens. It comes in bags from which you can pull out small amounts as needed. You can also use cotton stuffing, fleece, or any filling you prefer.

When it is necessary to fill small areas, such as the points of ears, etc., I use a crochet hook or the eraser end of a pencil to push the stuffing into place.

For quilts, you'll find batting in a variety of thicknesses and sizes. The information is printed on each bag, so you can buy the exact size for your project. The pillows shown in the book are made to standard sizes and can be filled with pillow forms, also available from Fairfield Processing, which are sold in fabric and five-and-ten-cent stores.

TRACING DESIGNS

Place a piece of tracing paper over the design or pattern in the book and copy each line with a marker, pen, or pencil. You can use this paper pattern to cut out the fabric pieces by pinning it directly onto the chosen fabric and cutting around the drawn lines. All pattern pieces are exact size. If seam allowance is needed, the directions with that project will instruct you to cut an extra ¼ inch all around the pattern.

TRANSFERRING DESIGNS AND PATTERNS

Many of the directions for each project will instruct you to make a template. In order to do this you will first transfer the design or pattern to template paper (see below). Use pencil to trace your design or pattern, then turn the tracing paper over and retrace the lines on the back. Place the tracing, with the original traced design up, over the template paper and rub a pencil over the outlines of the design. The design will appear faintly on the template paper. Remove the tracing and go over the template outline with a pencil or pen so you can see it more clearly. You can transfer the details by punching through the tracing paper with a ballpoint pen and making a mark on the fabric. This will tell you where to add embroidery details, for example.

A second method is to place a piece of carbon paper on the template paper, carbon side down, with the traced design on top. Using a pen, go over all pattern lines to transfer the design. Remove the carbon and tracing.

MAKING A TEMPLATE

A template is a pattern that is rigid and full size. It can be cut from cardboard, heavy paper, or acetate. The top of a box of stationery or a manila folder is good to use for making templates. Some templates used for quilting are made from sandpaper because it is the acceptable weight and won't slip on the fabric. I prefer the oak tag used for manila folders. It is inexpensive and easy to cut.

A template is used to trace the design elements when you are making more than one. It is more accurate than the paper pattern for making multiple patterns. It is also used to make appliqués. Transfer the pattern or design to the template material as described above. Cut out the design outline. Place the template on the fabric indicated for each project, draw around it as many times as required for the number of pieces needed, and then cut the fabric out along the drawn lines.

SEWING

Sewing pattern pieces in the right sequence makes a big difference in time and efficiency. Any hand or lap work such as stuffing and finishing openings should be done at one time. When sewing together pieces of fabric other than felt, use a ¼-inch seam allowance.

PATCHWORK

This is the traditional method for making quilts. It is the sewing together of fabric pieces to create an entire design. Sometimes the shapes form a geometric block. The blocks are then sewn together to make up a completed quilt.

QUILTING

Quilting is the means by which you sew layers of fabric and batting together to produce a padded fabric held together by stitching. It is warm and decorative and is generally the finishing step in appliqué and patchwork projects. Quilting is what makes a project interesting and gives it a textured look.

Hand-quilting: While most of the piecing for the top of a quilt is done on a sewing machine, the actual quilting is done by hand. This is what makes a quilt or pillow so appealing.

Before quilting you will baste and mark the fabric with the provided quilt pattern or follow the seam lines with stitches approximately ¼ inch on each side.

Begin by threading your needle. Keep the thread approximately as long as your arm. Give the knotted end of the thread a good tug and pull it through the backing fabric into the batting and through the top. Take small running stitches along the quilting lines.

Machine-quilting: This is easier, quicker, and often preferred for small projects such as Christmas ornaments, sachets, etc. Use thin quilt batting for machine-stitching and set the stitch length for a looser stitch, such as eight or nine stitches per inch.

Crafting in Quantity

No matter what technique you use, if you are making many of one project there are shortcuts for the preliminary work. The idea is to do the preparatory steps as efficiently as possible so that you can concentrate on the creative aspects of the project.

CUTTING OUT PATTERNS

Take the time to determine how you will place each pattern piece on the fabric to get the most from your material. When cutting out the front and back of a pattern, remember to cut one from the front of the fabric and one with the fabric turned to the wrong side. Or, cut one fabric piece from the folded fabric so you end up with two pieces in the correct position.

CUTTING OUT PATTERNS IN QUANTITY

When making ornaments, for example, you will probably be working in multiples. Use a large enough area to do all your cutting at once. Take time to study the patterns and determine how you will place each on the fabric to get the most from your material.

Mark the template on the back of all fabric and cut each pattern piece at once, rather than cutting all the pieces for one ornament before beginning another. Set the pieces in marked piles so you know what they are. When drawing and cutting around template shapes, consider making the same ornament in different colors for variety.

SEWING IN QUANTITY

Plan the steps carefully. If there are several pieces to a pattern, jot down the order in which they will be put together. You will find it easier to do the same step for all the ornaments, rather than finishing one project before beginning another. Mark all pattern pieces so you can do the same steps several times for different ornaments.

Plan your thread colors so that all stitching with one color can be done before changing thread. If you are making stuffed ornaments, cut and stitch all shapes, then add the stuffing, and finally do all hand-stitching at one time.

When cutting trimmings and attaching loops for hanging, cut and plan the placements before you begin. Sometimes it's possible to use one pattern for a bunch of ornaments and make each look different by adding a variety of interesting trimmings.

Basic Embroidery Stitches

Running stitch

1.

2.

Backstitch

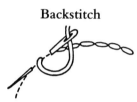

Feather stitch

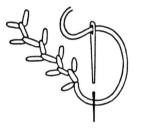

Blanket Stitch

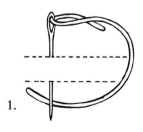
1.

Stem stitch

Satin stitch

Chain stitch

French knot

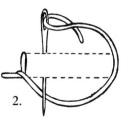

2.

3.

Lazy daisy

Continental

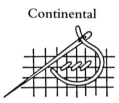

Cross-stitch

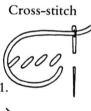
1.

2.

Crochet Basics

All crochet starts with a chain made up of a series of loops on a crochet hook. Unlike knitting, which is done on two, three, and sometimes four needles, crocheting is done on a single hook. Hooks come in various sizes. The size you use will depend on the yarn, pattern, and project.

The very simple stitches and techniques that follow will enable you to make all of the crocheted projects in this book, even if you've never crocheted before.

CHAIN STITCH (ch)

The beginning of every project in crochet is a row of a specific number of chain stitches. These are the basis of the piece, just as the cast-on row is the basis of a knit piece.

At the beginning of every row, an extra chain stitch (or stitches, in the case of double and treble crochet) is made. This is counted as the first stitch of the next row and is called the turning chain. In these instructions, each chain stitch is simply called a chain (ch). When a string of chain stitches is being discussed, it is known by the number of stitches, for example, "first ch-5" means the first group of chain stitches in a row.

1. Make a slip knot by taking yarn about 2 inches from the end and winding it once around your middle three fingers.
2. Draw a length of yarn through the loop around your fingers. Put this new loop on your crochet hook and pull tight.
3. With yarn wound over left-hand fingers, pass the hook under the yarn on index finger and catch a strand with the hook (Figure 1).
4. Draw the yarn through the loop already on the hook to make 1 chain stitch (ch) (Figure 2).

Repeat steps 3 and 4 for as many chain stitches as needed. If you hold the chain as close to the hook as possible with the thumb and index finger of your left hand, the chain will be even.

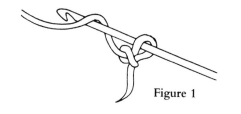

Figure 1

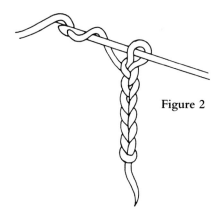

Figure 2

SINGLE CROCHET (sc)

1. After making the initial chain, insert the hook in the 2nd chain from the hook (the skipped chain is the turning chain) and bring the yarn over the hook from the back to the front (clockwise) (Figure 1). Draw the yarn through the chain so you have 2 loops on the hook, as shown in Figure 2.

2. Bring the yarn over the hook again and draw the hook with its 3rd loop through the 2 loops already on the hook. You have made 1 single crochet (sc).

3. Repeat steps 1 and 2 into each chain stitch across the row (Figure 3). At the end of the row, make 1 chain (ch 1) and turn the work around from right to left so the reverse side is facing you.

4. The turning chain stitch counts as the first stitch of the next row. Work the next single crochet by inserting the hook under the 2 top loops of the next stitch in the previous row. Continue by working a single crochet in each stitch across the row. Work a single crochet in the ch-1 (turning chain). Chain 1 and turn.

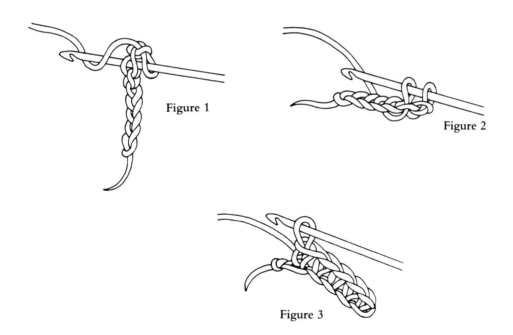

Figure 1

Figure 2

Figure 3

FASTENING OFF

At the end of all required rows or rounds, cut the yarn with a tail of 2 or 3 inches and draw it through the last loop at the end of the row. Pull tight and weave it into the fabric with a yarn needle. Sometimes the tail is used to sew pieces together. If this is the case, leave a tail that is long enough. Sometimes directions will say "break off," which is the same as fasten off.

DOUBLE CROCHET (dc)

1. After making the initial chain, bring the yarn over the hook and insert the hook, from front to back, into the 4th chain from the hook (the skipped chains are the turning chains) (Figure 1).
2. Yarn over hook. Draw through chain. There are now 3 loops on the hook (Figure 2).
3. Yarn over hook. Draw through 2 loops on the hook. There are now 2 loops on the hook (Figure 3).
4. Yarn over hook. Draw the yarn through the last 2 loops on the hook (Figure 4). One double crochet (dc) is completed.

Yarn over hook, insert hook into next chain stitch, and repeat steps 2, 3, and 4.

Repeat into each chain stitch across the row. At the end of the row, make 3 chains (ch-3) and turn the work around from right to left so the reverse side is facing you.

The turning chain counts as the first stitch of the next row. Work the next double crochet by bringing the yarn over the hook and inserting the hook under the 2 top loops of the next stitch in the previous row. Continue by working a double crochet in each stitch across the row. Work a double crochet in the 3rd stitch of the ch-3 (turning chain). Chain 3 and turn.

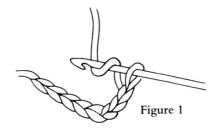

Figure 1

Figure 2

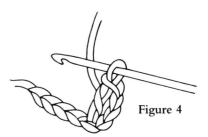

Figure 3

Figure 4

14

HALF DOUBLE CROCHET (hdc)

1. After making the initial chain, bring the yarn over the hook and insert the hook, from front to back, into the 3rd chain from the hook (the skipped chains are the turning chains) (Figure 1).

2. Yarn over hook. Draw through chain. There are now 3 loops on the hook (Figure 2).

3. Yarn over hook (Figure 3). Draw through all 3 loops. One half double crochet (hdc) is completed (Figure 4). Yarn over hook, insert hook into next chain stitch, and repeat steps 2 and 3.

Repeat into each chain stitch across the row. At the end of the row, make 2 chains (ch 2) and turn the work around from right to left so the reverse side is facing you.

The turning chain counts as the first stitch of the next row. Work the next half double crochet by bringing the yarn over the hook and inserting the hook under the 2 top loops of the next stitch of the previous row. Continue by working a half double crochet in each stitch across the row. Work a half double crochet in the ch-2 turning chain. Chain 2 and turn.

Figure 1

Figure 2

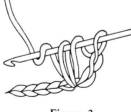

Figure 3

Figure 4

TREBLE OR TRIPLE CROCHET (tr)

1. After making the initial chain, wind the yarn around the hook twice (Figure 1) and insert the hook, from front to back, into the 5th chain from the hook (the skipped chains are the turning chains).

2. Yarn over hook. Draw through chain. There are now 4 loops on the hook.

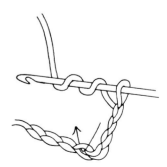

Figure 1

15

3. Yarn over hook. Draw through 2 loops (Figure 2). There are now 3 loops on the hook.

4. Yarn over hook. Draw through 2 loops (Figure 3). There are now 2 loops on the hook.

5. Yarn over hook. Draw through the last 2 loops (Figure 4). One triple crochet (tr) is completed (Figure 5). Wind the yarn around the hook twice, insert the hook into the next chain stitch, and repeat steps 2, 3, 4, and 5.

Repeat into each chain stitch across the row. At the end of the row, make 4 chains (ch 4) and turn the work around from right to left so the reverse side is facing you.

The turning chains count as the first stitch of the next row. Work the next triple crochet by winding the yarn around the hook twice and inserting the hook under the 2 top loops of the next stitch in the previous row. Continue by working a triple crochet in each stitch across the row. Work a triple crochet in the ch-4 turning chain. Chain 4 and turn.

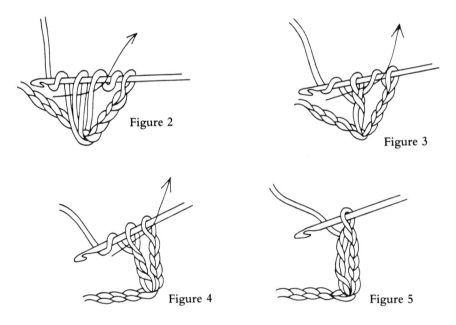

Figure 2

Figure 3

Figure 4

Figure 5

DOUBLE TREBLE OR TRIPLE CROCHET (dtr)

1. After making the initial chain, wind the yarn around the hook 3 times and insert the hook, from front to back, into the 6th chain from the hook (the skipped chains are the turning chains).

2. Yarn over hook. Draw through the chain. There are now 5 loops on the hook.

3. Yarn over hook. Draw through 2 loops. There are now 4 loops on the chain.

4. Repeat 3 more times until there is one loop left on the hook. One double triple crochet (dtr) is completed.

SLIP STITCH (sl st)

Insert the hook into the chain (Figure 1). Yarn over hook. Draw through both the chain and the loop on the hook in one motion (Figure 2). One slip stitch (sl) is completed (Figure 3). A slip stitch is used to join a chain in order to form a ring.

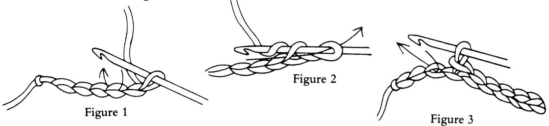

Figure 1

Figure 2

Figure 3

WORKING IN SPACES

In crochet work that is lacy and contains openwork, often a stitch in the preceding row is skipped and you will be instructed to chain across the gap. Sometimes the pattern tells you to work stitches in a space instead of in a stitch. In that case, insert your hook through the gap or space (sp) rather than through a stitch in the preceding row. Often several stitches are worked in 1 space, as a way of increasing stitches.

INCREASING SINGLE CROCHET (inc)

When a pattern calls for an increase of a single crochet, work 2 stitches in 1 stitch (Figure 1).

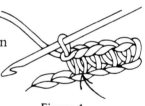

Figure 1

DECREASING SINGLE CROCHET (dec)

When a pattern calls for a decrease of a single crochet, draw up a loop in 1 stitch, then draw up a loop in the next stitch so there are 3 loops on your hook (Figure 1). Yarn over hook and draw through all 3 loops at once (Figure 2).

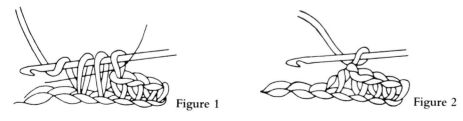

Figure 1

Figure 2

WORKING EVEN

This means to continue in the same manner without either increasing or decreasing stitches.

CROCHET ABBREVIATIONS

beg—beginning
ch—chain
dc—double crochet
dec—decrease
hdc—half double crochet
inc—increase
lp—loop
pat—pattern
rep—repeat
rnd—round
sc—single crochet
sk—skip

sl st—slip stitch
sp—space
st—stitch
sts—stitches
tog—together
tr—treble or triple crochet
yo—yarn over hook
★—repeat what comes after
( )—work directions in parentheses as many times as specified after parentheses. For example: (dc 1) 3 times.

KNITTING ABBREVIATIONS

beg—beginning
CC—contrasting color
dec—decrease
inc—increase
k—knit
lp—loop
MC—main color
p—purl
pat—pattern

rem—remaining
rep—repeat
sk—skip
sl—slip
sl st—slip stitch
st—stitch
sts—stitches
tog—together
yo—yarn over needle

Knitting Basics

Knitting is based on two basic stitches, knit and purl. From these you can make all kinds of knitted projects. By combining these two stitches in different variations, you will be able to create a simple garment or as elaborate a project as you can imagine.

The knitting projects in this book confine themselves to a basic knit and purl stitch to produce what is known as a stockinette pattern. The following will teach you what you need to know in order to make the knitting projects in this book.

CASTING ON

To begin any project, you will need to cast a specified number of stitches onto your needles. This becomes the base on which you will work your first row of knitting. When counting rows, do not count the cast-on row.

1. Start by making a slip knot, leaving a tail of yarn about 3 inches long. Place the loop of the knot on the left-hand needle (Figure 1). (Left-handers should reverse these and all other instructions.) Use your right-hand needle to make the stitches to cast onto the left-hand needle as follows.

2. Wrap the yarn around your right ring finger to create tension, and insert the right-hand needle from front to back through the loop on the left-hand needle. The two needles are now in the loop, with the right-hand needle behind the left.

3. Bring the yarn clockwise around the right-hand needle. With the right-hand needle, pull the yarn through the loop on the left needle (Figure 2).

4. Bring the tip of the left-hand needle from right to left through the loop on the right needle.

5. Withdraw the right-hand needle, pull the yarn slightly taut, and you have 2 stitches on the left needle (Figure 3). Continue to do this until you have the required number of stitches.

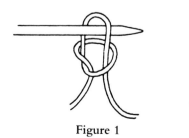

Figure 1

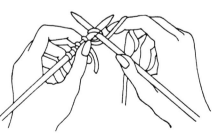

Figure 2

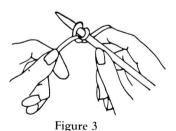

Figure 3

KNIT STITCH

1. Hold the needle with cast-on stitches in your left hand, with the yarn around your left forefinger. Insert the right-hand needle from front to back through the first loop on the left-hand needle as shown in Figure 1.
2. Bring the yarn under and over the point of the right needle (Figure 2). Draw the yarn through the loop with the point of the needle (Figure 3).
3. Use your right forefinger to push the tip of the left needle down to let the loop on the left needle slip off. You now have 1 stitch on your right needle (Figure 4). Work across the row in this way.

   After finishing a row of knitting, transfer the right-hand needle to the left hand and the left-hand needle to the right hand, turning the needles also (the points always face each other), and continue the next row in the same way, always taking the stitches from the left to the right needle.

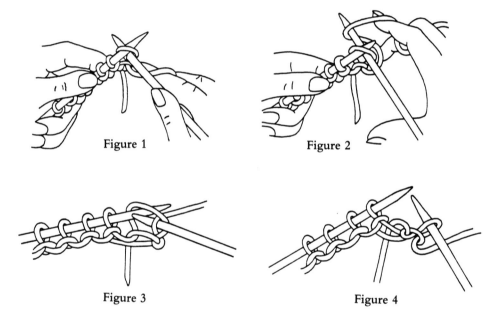

Figure 1

Figure 2

Figure 3

Figure 4

PURL STITCH

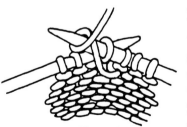

Figure 1

1. With cast-on stitches on your left-hand needle, insert the point of your right-hand needle from right to left through the front of the first stitch. With the yarn in front of your work (rather than in back as with the knit stitch), wind it over and around the needle's point (Figure 1).
2. Draw the yarn back through the stitch and let the loop on the left needle slip off the needle. Your first purl stitch is now on your right-hand needle.

STOCKINETTE STITCH

Work 1 row with the knit stitch. Purl each stitch in the next row. Continue to knit 1 row and purl the next row for a stockinette fabric. The pattern on the front of the work is that of interlocking V's. The back of the fabric looks like a tighter version of the garter stitch (knit every row).

INCREASING A STITCH

This means that you will be making 2 stitches from 1. Knit the first stitch as usual, but do not drop the stitch off the left-hand needle. Bring the right-hand needle behind the left-hand needle and insert it from right to left into the back of the same stitch. Make another stitch by winding yarn under and over the right-hand needle (knit stitch). Slip the stitch off the left-hand needle (Figure 2).

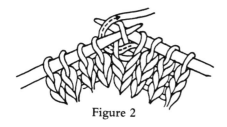

Figure 2

DECREASING A STITCH

If you are decreasing stitches, to shape a raglan armhole, for example, you will be knitting or purling 2 stitches together to form 1 stitch. In a pattern the direction will be given as k 2 tog or p 2 tog (Figure 3).

On the right side of your work, knit 2 stitches together as if they were 1. When decreasing a purl stitch, work on the back side and purl 2 stitches together.

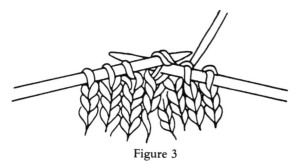

Figure 3

BINDING OFF

1. Knit the first 2 stitches. Insert the left-hand needle from left to the right through the front of the first (the right-most) stitch (Figure 1).

2. Lift the first stitch over the second stitch and the tip of the right-hand needle (Figure 2). (Use your left hand to push the tip of the right-hand needle back while pulling the stitch through.) Let the lifted stitch drop, and you now have 1 stitch on the right-hand needle (Figure 3). Knit another stitch and lift the right-most stitch over the next as before. Repeat this across the row until 1 stitch is left.

3. Loosen the remaining loop on the right-hand needle and withdraw the needle. Cut the yarn, leaving 2 or 3 inches, and pull this tail through the loop (Figure 4). Tighten the knot.

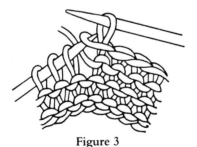

Figure 1

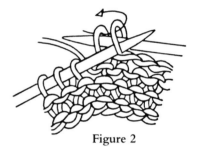

Figure 2

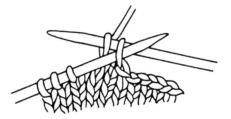

Figure 3

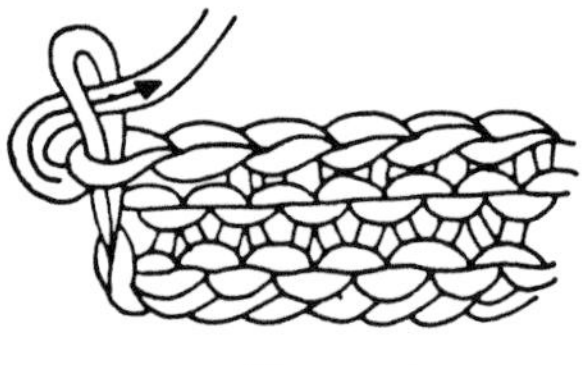

Figure 4

Santa's Gift Bag

All of these projects have been designed for quick-and-easy crafting to keep those hectic days before the holidays fun, not frustrating. There's a gift here for everyone on your list, from a darling knitted baby hat and scarf to elegant white quilted pillows for a favorite friend or relative. You might even like to make some of the projects for yourself. When you look through this chapter keep in mind that it's much easier to make double of a project than to finish one and start over again. If you especially like one of the projects and want to make it for yourself, buy enough material to make two and plan each step accordingly.

Swan Lake Pillow

Tartan plaid fabric is especially popular and looks festive for the holidays. But it will go on looking quite lovely all year long and makes a beautiful background for our white swan appliqués. Each has a red bow tie and the pillow is trimmed with matching red piping. The finished size is 16 × 16 inches and takes a standard pillow form.

MATERIALS

Small piece of red fabric
14 × 14-inch piece of white fabric
  (not too thin)
½ yard green tartan fabric
2 yards red piping
16-inch pillow form

Red and white thread
12- to 14-inch zipper (if desired)
Tracing paper
Heavy paper, such as manila
  folder

DIRECTIONS

1. Begin by tracing the swan and bow patterns. Transfer to the heavy paper to make templates (see page 8). Cut out each piece.
2. Place the swan template in one corner of the white fabric and draw around the outline. Draw 4 swans in this way.
3. Next, place the bow pattern on the red fabric and draw around 4 times.
4. Cut out all pieces. No seam allowance is needed as the appliqués will be zigzag-stitched to the background.
5. Cut two tartan squares, each 16½ × 16½ inches.
6. Refer to Assembly Diagram and arrange the swans on one piece of tartan. Pin each one to the background. Pin a bow on the neck of each one so they are all identically positioned.
7. Using white thread and a zigzag stitch on your sewing machine, stitch around each swan, skipping over the red fabric.
8. Next, using red thread, zigzag-stitch around each bow.

To Finish

1. With right sides facing and raw edges aligned, start in the center of one side of the pillow top and pin the piping all around with raw edges meeting.
2. Use a zipper foot on your machine and stitch all around as close to piping as possible.
3. With right sides facing and raw edges aligned, pin the back tartan piece to the pillow top all around 3 sides and 4 corners.

4. Using the piping stitches as a guide, stitch around three sides and four corners of the pillow.

5. Clip corners and turn right side out. Press. If desired, insert a zipper into the open side of the pillow. If not, turn the seam allowance of the raw edges to the inside and press.

6. Insert the pillow form and slip-stitch opening closed.

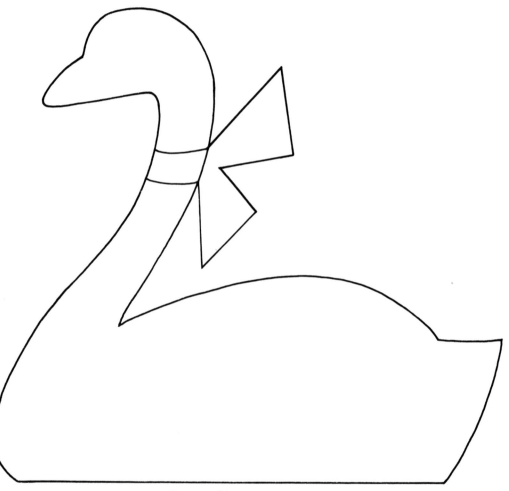

Swan and bow patterns

Assembly diagram

Scotty Towels

It's easy to make ordinary towels look special for gift giving by adding a festive appliqué. Here we used blue tartan plaid for the body of the scotty dogs and added a green bow around each neck. A band of tartan makes a trim edge and each element is outlined with a zigzag stitch for a crisp finish. Consider making these for your own guest bathroom. They will add a dash of holiday cheer. See photo on page 25.

MATERIALS

Red hand towels
Small amount of green fabric
¼ yard tartan fabric

Navy blue thread
Tracing paper

DIRECTIONS

1. Trace the scotty dog and bow patterns, each 2 times.
2. Pin the scotty pattern to the tartan and cut 2.
3. Pin the bow pattern to the green fabric and cut 2.
4. Cut 2 strips of tartan, each 1 inch by the width of the hand towel.
5. Position each strip approximately 3 inches from the bottom edge of each towel and pin in place. Turn the raw edges at each end under and pin to the towel.
6. Center each scotty approximately 1½ inches above the tartan strip on each towel and pin in place. Pin a green bow on each dog's neck.
7. Using a zigzag stitch and navy blue thread, stitch along the top and bottom edges of each strip and across each end.
8. Zigzag-stitch around the raw edges of the appliqués.

Scotty and bow patterns

Wee Wraps

All it takes is a basic knowledge of knitting to create this adorable hat and scarf for an infant. The hat will fit from newborn to 18 months. Our friend Else Knudson from Norway made this for us, based on a Scandinavian design. Else says that blue and white is a favorite color combination for knitwear and that everyone in her country wears handknit sweaters. "We call the little heart-shaped stitches 'flies,' " she says. Last year Else came to Nantucket to spend a year as an *au pair*. During the year she made many craft projects that we designed in the studio.

MATERIALS

Sport-weight yarn (1.75 oz./50 gm. balls): 3 balls white and 1 ball blue
Knitting needles: *For scarf:* #4/3.5 mm or size needed to obtain gauge
   For hat: 14-inch-long #4/3.5 mm or size needed to obtain gauge

GAUGE

5 sts = 1 inch
6 rows = 1 inch

Scarf

DIRECTIONS

Using white yarn cast on 28 stitches. Working the entire scarf in knit 2, purl 2, use the following color sequence:
   1 row white
   3 rows blue
   11 rows white
   3 rows blue
Change to white and work 28 inches ending with:
   3 rows blue
   11 rows white
   3 rows blue
   1 row white
   Bind off.

To Finish

Fringe (worked across each short edge of the scarf): Cut 2 strands of blue and 2 strands of white, each 4½ inches long. Fold in half and draw loop end through side edge of one end of the scarf. Pull the loose ends through the loop and draw tightly.

Attach 2 strands of blue and 2 strands of white in every 4th stitch. There will be 13 tassels at each end. Trim the ends so they are even.

Hat

DIRECTIONS

With white yarn cast on 56 sts. Work 1 row knit 2, purl 2; then change to blue yarn and work 3 rows knit 2, purl 2; change to white and work 3 rows knit 2, purl 2. Follow the color sequence in Figure 1 for each of the next 4 rows and work in stockinette stitch (knit 1 row, purl 1 row). Continue in stockinette st and work as follows:

3 rows white, decreasing 1 st by knitting 2 together in the first row
3 rows blue
1 row white

Refer to Figure 2 for color sequence until you have a total of 7 inches, or desired length.

Using white yarn work a row knitting every 2 sts together. Fasten off leaving a 12-inch tail. Thread through the remaining 26 sts and gather. Secure and sew the side seams together.

To Finish

Pompon. Combining white and blue yarn, wind the strands around your hand several times to create a thickness of the desired size. Slide the loop off your hand and, using the tail at the top of the hat, tie around the center of the loops. Make a secure knot. Cut the ends of the loops and fluff up into a pompon.

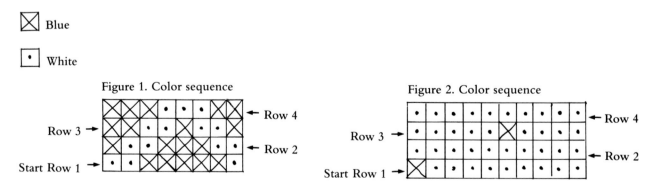

⊠ Blue

· White

Figure 1. Color sequence

Row 3 →
← Row 4
← Row 2
Start Row 1 →

Figure 2. Color sequence

Row 3 →
← Row 4
← Row 2
Start Row 1 →

Flowers and Bows Afghan Set

This baby coverlet is made up of four strips of six squares each. Each square in the strip is approximately 5 × 6 inches and squares of afghan stitch and double crochet are alternated. It looks as though it's been made of 24 squares stitched together, but strips are much easier to put together when completed. The finished size is approximately 30 × 34 inches, including the picot edging. The illustration is created with a counted cross-stitch design worked on top of the afghan stitch.

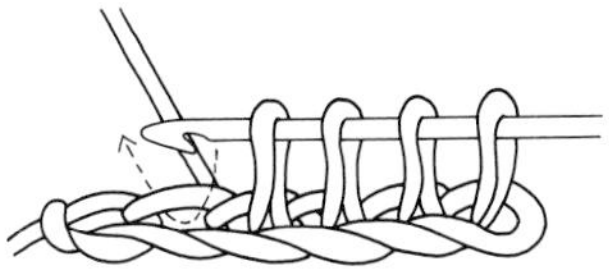

Figure 1

MATERIALS

Unger's Utopia 4-ply acrylic yarn
   (3.5 oz./100 gm. balls)—5 skeins white,
   1 skein each of peach and blue
Stuffing

Yarn needle
Afghan hook: Aero 5.5
Crochet hook: H/8 (5 mm)
or size needed to obtain gauge

GAUGE

3 sts = 1 inch
3 rows = 1 inch

Figure 2

DIRECTIONS

Afghan Stitch

Row 1: Draw up a loop in each stitch of chain, leaving all lps on hook as shown in Figure 1. Take lps off as follows: Yarn over hook, draw through 1 lp, ★ yo, draw through 2 lps, repeat from ★ across the row as shown in Figure 2. The lp remaining on the hook counts as the first lp of the next row (see Figure 3).
Row 2: Skip the first upright bar and draw up a lp in the next and each remaining upright bar, leaving all lps on the hook. Take lps off in the same way as Row 1. Repeat only Row 2 for desired length (Figure 4).

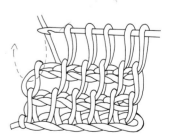

Figure 3

Strips 1 and 2

With white yarn, ch 25. Using the afghan hook, crochet with the afghan st for 18 rows or 6 inches. Change to the #8 crochet hook.
Row 1: ★ Double crochet across 25 sts.
Row 2: Single crochet back.
Rep from ★ 8 times. Alternate and rep these 2 squares 2 more times. You now have a strip of 6 squares. Crochet another strip in the same way.

Figure 4

Strips 3 and 4

Ch 25 sts. Alternate by starting these strips with the double-crochet square first for 18 rows, then the afghan-stitch square for 18 rows. Continue until you have worked 6 squares in this way.

To Finish

Arrange the strips so they make a checkerboard design. To finish the edges of the two middle strips, scallop along the long edge on each side as follows: *Scallop stitch.* 3 dc in the first st, ch 1, ★ 3 dc in same st. Sk 1 st, sc in the next st, sk 1 st and rep all along strip from ★ to the end. With the yarn needle, sew the strips together, attaching at the peak of each scallop. Thread the yarn through the sts between the scallops so it doesn't show.
Edging. Using the crochet hook and the peach-colored yarn, sc 1 row around the afghan. Change to white and sc 2 rows around the afghan edge. Change to peach and, using the same directions as for the scallops between strips, scallop around the afghan. Scallop all around once more and, at the peak of each scallop in the first scallop row, crochet each scallop ★ 3 dc, ch 1, 3 dc. Between scallops work 1 dc. Rep from ★ all around. Bind off.

Cross-Stitch Embroidery

Each upright bar across the row of an afghan st is counted as 1 st. Follow the chart and count upright bars. There are 2 holes formed by the afghan st *after* each upright bar. Each square on the chart represents a square on the afghan.

Working from left to right, join the color on the wrong side at the lower hole and work across the next upright bar to the upper hole. Then bring the needle through the lower hole directly below as shown in Figure 5. Continue on the number of stitches for the color being used. Then work from the right to the left to form an X. Do not pull the yarn too tight.

Refer to the assembly diagram for placement of each design. Using the blue yarn for the ribbon bows and peach for the flowers, follow the charts and work the design in cross-stitch on the afghan-stitch squares only.

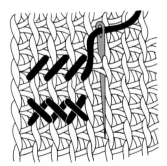

Figure 5. Cross-stitch over afghan stitch

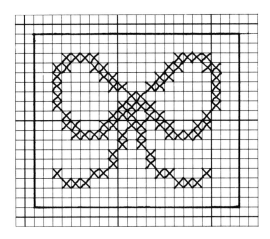

Afghan

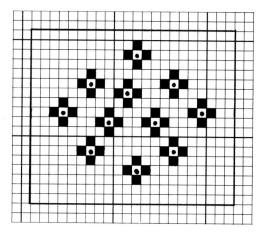

■ Peach

⊡ Yellow

⊠ Blue

Assembly Diagram

	Bow		Flowers
Bow		Flowers	
	Flowers		Bow
Flowers		Bow	
	Bow		Flowers
Bow		Flowers	

Pillow

The pillow is a 10-inch square made entirely with the afghan stitch. Make 2. When fastening off, leave a long enough tail to stitch the 2 pieces together around the edges.

Follow chart to cross-stitch the design on the front of one square. Stitch back and front pillow pieces together leaving one side open. Fill with stuffing and stitch opening closed. Beginning at one corner, follow the scallop st directions for edging all around the pillow.

Pillow

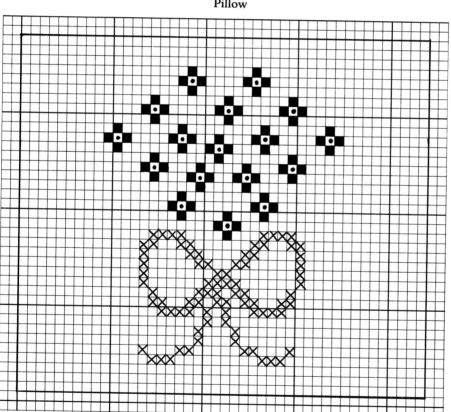

Santa Bottle Cover

Make a jolly Santa face to cover a gift bottle for the holidays. It's easy to crochet this project with leftover yarn and if you want to make it for yourself, create a centerpiece around the Santa over an empty bottle.

MATERIALS

Knitting worsted-weight yarn: 1 oz. each of red, tan, and white; small amount of white and black

3-inch-long piece of cardboard ¾ inches wide

Crochet hooks: #9 (5.5 mm) or size needed for correct gauge #1 (1.5 mm) for facial features

GAUGE

4 sts = 1 inch
4 rows = 1 inch

DIRECTIONS

With tan yarn chain 48 and join in a circle. Single crochet around and around for 5 inches. Bind off. (Put hook through complete stitch). With white yarn, *double loop stitch* all around as follows: Pull up yarn in st to make 2 loops on the hook, ★ wrap yarn around the ¾-inch cardboard and pull through the same st (3 lps on hook), yarn over hook and through the first lp on the hook (there will be 3 lps on the hook). Repeat from ★ once more in the same st, yo and through all 4 sts on the hook. (Each double loop st is an increase st.)

Hair

Crochet 1 row of *single loop stitch* as follows: Work as double loop st, omitting the repeat. Crochet another row of double loop st and bind off. Turn inside out so that the lps hang down.

Hat

Attach red yarn. Sc 48 sts around. Continue for 6 rows of sc, picking up *just the back* of each stitch. Decrease 1 st every row at the back for 24 rows as follows: Pull up a lp in 1 st, then pull up a lp in the next st so there are 3 lps on your hook. Yo hook and draw through all 3 lps at once. When all rows are complete, bind off.

Tassel

Wind white yarn 10 times around the 3-inch length of cardboard. Knot one end of lps together and cut the other end. Attach to the top of the hat.

Beard

With white, ch 9 inches. Single loop st in each st. Bind off. Refer to Figure 1 for positioning of the beard. Use a needle and white thread to attach the beard, creating a "frame" for Santa's face.

Face

With #1 hook and red yarn, ch 5 sts for the nose. Join in a circle. Using black yarn ch 4 sts for the eyes. Join in a circle. Through the hole formed in the center sc 5 sts. Bind off. Attach to the face as shown in Figure 1. To make the mouth, use the #9 hook and ch 10 sts. Bind off and stitch in position on the face.

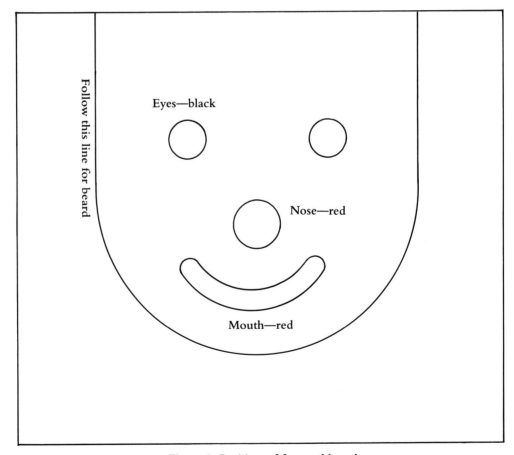

Figure 1. Position of face and beard

Snowflake Cross-Stitch Pillows

Make these handsome pillows using a background of Hopscotch plaid Aida cloth and cross-stitch a snowflake design in the center of each. These were made by my friend Suzi Peterson who says they are easy and fun to make. Each pillow is 14 × 14 inches and the blue snowflake design will look good for the holidays as well as the rest of the year.

MATERIALS

1 piece of blue and white Hopscotch 14-count Aida cloth (available in craft stores) for each pillow
1 skein embroidery floss of each color: dark blue, medium blue, and light blue
Embroidery needle
Small embroidery hoop (optional, but handy)
2 yards white or blue piping
½ yard of muslin or solid color for the backing
14-inch pillow form or stuffing
12-inch zipper (optional)

DIRECTIONS

How To Cross-Stitch

1. Cut a length of embroidery floss approximately as long as your arm.
2. Separate the 6 strands of floss and then rejoin 3. This keeps the floss from knotting and tangling. Thread the needle with the joined strands.
3. Find the center of the charted design. Fold the fabric in half horizontally and vertically to find the center of the fabric. Once you've located the center of the design on the chart, count up to the top row and out to the first X to find your starting point. Do the same on your fabric. Each square on the charted design represents a corresponding square on the fabric. You are now ready to begin working your stitches in horizontal rows.
4. If using an embroidery hoop, secure the area to be embroidered in the hoop. Tighten the hoop so the fabric is as taut as possible. This makes it easier to insert the needle into the fabric holes, and the stitches will be consistently neat. Even tension produces beautifully perfect work.
5. Do not make a knot on one end of the floss as you would for regular sewing. Locate the first square and insert your needle into one fabric hole from the underside. Pull it through until you have a 2-inch tail remaining, which will later be secured under the first few stitches.

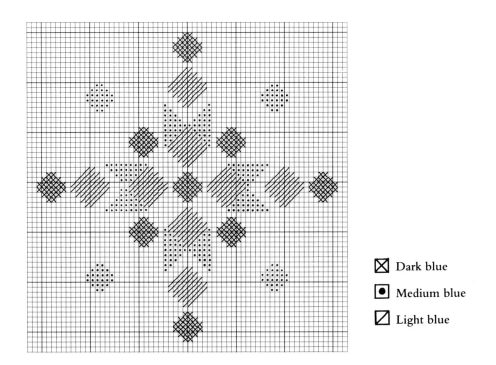

☒ Dark blue

⊡ Medium blue

◩ Light blue

6. Reinsert the needle through the hole diagonally to the right, across the first square on the front of the fabric. Continue to do this, working diagonally across the row, using the same color as indicated on the chart.

7. When you have completed a section of stitches slanted left to right, cross back to make each stitch into an X. Each time you run out of floss, weave the last bit under a few stitches on the underside to secure the work. When working on a small area, such as the points of the snowflake, complete and end the floss and start again in another section rather than drag floss over a wide unworked area, where it might show through the fabric.

When the design has been completed, remove from the hoop. Place the work face down on a padded surface and, using a damp press cloth over the work, steam-press the fabric.

To Finish

1. With right sides facing and raw edges aligned, pin the piping to the front of the pillow top making sure that the raw ends meet in the middle of the lower edge.

2. Using a zipper foot on your machine, stitch around.

3. Cut a backing piece 14½ × 14½ inches. With right sides facing and raw edges aligned, pin the backing and front together with the piping between.

4. Using the piping stitches as a guide, stitch around 3 sides and 4 corners.

5. Clip corners and turn pillow right side out. Attach zipper to open side if desired.

6. Insert the pillow form or stuff fully. Slip-stitch opening closed if no zipper has been used.

Plastic Canvas Pins

It's easy to make striking needlepoint gift tags with plastic canvas. If you add a pin backing before tying it to the package, it can become a gift after the package is opened. Make some for tree ornaments, others as luggage tags and bookmarks. Plastic canvas, which is available in craft and some fabric shops, makes this a quick-and-easy project because the squares are large and there's no blocking necessary. You can work a counted cross-stitch or the continental stitch (see page 11), which is half a cross-stitch. Plastic canvas is a lot of fun and you'll think of all sorts of uses for it once you get started. It even comes in colors so you don't have to fill in the entire background, but it's nicer if you do. I made all of these in just one evening!

MATERIALS

1 sheet of plastic canvas for all projects
Leftover lengths of red, green, and blue 4-ply acrylic yarn
Yarn needle
Scraps of fusible felt for backing (or glue plain felt to the back)
White craft glue if plain felt is used
Pin backings
Ribbon for bookmarks

DIRECTIONS

1. Starting three or four rows up from the bottom edge and in as many rows from one side edge, follow the chart for placement of each stitch and color for your initials or letters to spell a word.
2. Find the starting point for the first stitch. Leave an inch of yarn at the back of the canvas and bring the needle up through the first hole, then down through the diagonal hole to create a slant. If you want to fill in more of the area, bring the needle up through the opposite hole of the square and down again to form an X. You have completed the first stitch of the first letter to correspond to the stitch indicated on the chart.
3. Continue to follow the chart in order to fill in the letters. Work the background in the color of your choice. You can create a one-, two-, or three-row border all around depending on how large you want the tag to be. This can be determined as you go along. Complete one row, then another, stopping whenever you like the look of the project. I found that one or two rows of background were sufficient.

4. When finished, cut the square as neatly as possible and work an overcast stitch all around to finish the edges. You can use the same color as the background or a contrasting color.

To Finish

1. Cut a piece of felt same size as the needlepoint piece and fuse to the back with a hot iron. If you can't find iron-on felt, glue a piece of plain felt to the back of the needlepoint.
2. Stitch or glue the pin backing in the center of the back if desired.
3. Thread a loop of yarn through the center top of the tag and tie to a package or hang on the tree.
4. To make a bookmark: Cut a length of ribbon approximately 8 inches and place one end on the back of the needlepoint. Cut a piece of felt same size as the needlepoint piece and fuse or glue to the back of the canvas with the ribbon between.

Alphabet chart

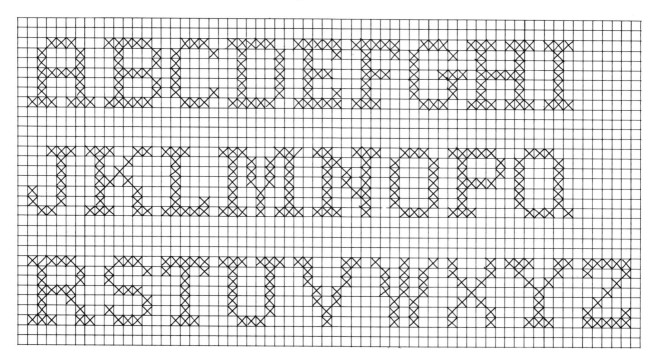

White Quilted Pillows

These soft, delicate pillows will be appreciated by anyone. They are especially nice in the bedroom and would be equally pretty on a living room sofa. The quilting can be done with white thread for a very subtle effect or with pink so the quilted design is more prominent. We designed these patterns in the studio and my grandmother, Ruth Linsley, quilted them for us. The finished size is 14 × 14 inches, which is perfect for a throw pillow.

MATERIALS (for 2 pillows)

1 yard 45-inch-wide white fabric or bleached muslin
Pink or white thread
4 yards white piping
2 pillow forms 14 × 14 inches or stuffing

2 pieces of batting, each 14 × 14 inches
12-inch zipper (optional)
Tracing paper
Quilter's water-soluble marking pen

DIRECTIONS

1. Cut 4 squares, each 14½ × 14½ inches, from the white fabric.
2. Using a ballpoint pen or marker, trace each of the quilting patterns, which represent half the pattern. Turn the tracing and retrace to complete the pattern.
3. Place one of the white squares over one of the patterns and, using the quilter's marker, trace the pattern onto the fabric. Repeat with the second pattern. If it is difficult to see the design through the fabric, tape the tracing with the fabric on top to a windowpane. The light will enable you to see the pattern more clearly and you'll have no trouble transferring it to the fabric.

To Quilt

1. With the design side up, pin the marked fabric to one batting square.
2. To quilt refer to page 9. Using small running stitches, follow the drawn lines to quilt each of the pillow tops. Remove the pins.

To Finish

1. With right sides facing and raw edges aligned, pin the piping around the pillow top so the raw ends meet in the center of the bottom edge.
2. Use a zipper foot on your machine to stitch around as close to piping as possible.

3. With right sides facing and raw edges aligned, pin the backing to the pillow top with the piping between.

4. Using the piping stitches as a guide, stitch around 3 sides and 4 corners, leaving 1 side open for turning.

5. Clip corners and turn right side out. Press from the wrong side.

6. Insert zipper if desired or turn raw edges to inside and press. Insert pillow form or stuff, making sure to push stuffing into each corner before filling completely.

7. Slip-stitch opening closed if no zipper has been attached.

Center

One-half quilting pattern

Center

Center

One-half quilting pattern

Center

50

Elegant Boxes

Fabric-covered hatboxes are extremely popular and are used to hold lingerie, yarn, mementos, stationery items, and much more. They offer a way to be organized by holding things neatly on closet shelves, for example, and they're also pretty accessories in a room. Printed fabrics, wrapping paper, and wallpaper can be used to cover ordinary wooden, metal, or plastic boxes as well as cardboard gift boxes. They can hold gifts or become the gifts. If you have leftover wallpaper you can coordinate the accessories by covering boxes to match.

Self-sticking Contact paper is easy to use and there's a wide variety of designs that include tiny florals, country cross-stitch symbols, and the Disney characters for children's projects. Choosing the right coverings is fun and creative. Add trimming, such as braid, ribbon, or a wallpaper border, to give each one a finishing touch. We use the boxes shown here to hold art and craft supplies in the studio.

Fabric-Covered Round and Oval Boxes

MATERIALS

A variety of boxes
Enough fabric to cover inside and out (including bottom)
Rubber cement (available in art stores)

Tools: scissors, pencil, tape measure

DIRECTIONS

1. Measure the circumference of the box. Add 1 inch to the length and width and mark this on the back of the fabric.
2. Cut this piece as one continuous strip.
3. Next, cut a band to go around the lid in the same way, 1 inch longer and wider than actual measurement.

4. Adding ½ inch all around, mark and cut a piece for the top and bottom.

5. Cut the lining pieces in the same way to the exact measurement with no extra added.

6. Apply a coat of rubber cement to the back of each piece of fabric and set aside to dry.

7. Apply rubber cement to all surfaces of the box and let dry.

Attaching Material

Note: When using rubber cement you can't lift and reapply if you make a mistake, so do this right the first time or you'll need rubber cement remover to lift a piece and begin again. (Excess rubber cement can be removed easily when dry by rubbing over it with a gum eraser, available in art supply stores, or with your fingers.)

1. Attach the top and bottom pieces first. Make evenly spaced cuts all around the excess fabric that extends over the edges. Press the excess material around the edges and down over the sides or up onto the sides from the bottom.

2. Next, attach bands to the top and bottom so the extra inch folds to the inside.
3. Apply rubber cement to the inside pieces and to the inside of the box and inside the lid. Let all dry thoroughly before attaching.
4. Attach trim, ribbon, rickrack, or braid if desired.

Paper-Covered Rectangular Boxes

MATERIALS

A variety of boxes
Pretty paper
White craft glue or rubber cement

Trimmings (optional)
Tools: scissors, pencil, ruler,
  single-edge razor blade

DIRECTIONS

1. Measure all sides of the box, including the top, bottom, and inside.
2. Cut corresponding paper pieces for each area of the box. It's a good idea to identify each piece, such as "left inside," "left outside," etc.
3. If using rubber cement, apply to all pieces and set aside to dry thoroughly. Apply rubber cement to all areas of the box and let dry. If using white craft glue, apply to one piece at a time and set in position, while tacky, on the box.
4. If using rubber cement, carefully attach each piece.
5. When the entire box is covered, inside and out, you can trim any excess paper with a clean, sharp razor blade.
6. Glue trimming around the edges where the top and bottom come together, or around the top and bottom edges as you see fit.

Mini Wreaths

Rummage through your scrap basket, desk drawer, craft box, even the kitchen catch-all drawer for odds and ends to use for wreath trimmings. You'll be surprised at how creative you can be. Miniature wreaths are sold in craft and notions stores and can be used as tree decorations or small gifts. We make at least a dozen every Christmas for taking along when we visit during the holidays.

In the Nantucket studio, we decorate with small shells gathered on the beach in the summertime. It's a reminder that we live on an island. Perhaps there's something particular to the place where you live that can be used to personalize your wreath.

Consider using snapshots, trimmed to fit around the wreath. This is an especially nice gift for a child to send to Grandma and Grandpa. Other suggestions for trimmings are buttons, ribbons, dried flowers, tiny pinecones, novelty magnets, sequins, star stickers, artificial holly, and small Christmas gift tags.

MATERIALS

Small wreath
Ribbon or yarn for hanging
Variety of trimmings

White craft glue or hot-glue gun
(available in craft stores or five-and-dimes)

DIRECTIONS

1. Plan the elements and how they will fit around the wreath.
2. If you are using paper items it's easy to attach them with white craft glue. However, for heavier items such as magnets, large buttons, etc., the hot-glue gun is better. If you're decorating a wreath with bulky items that don't have a flat surface, such as shells, the glue gun works best. When arranging the shells, let each overlap the next one as you glue it in place.
3. Let all elements dry thoroughly. Glue a pretty taffeta or lace bow to the top and thread the hanging loop through the center of the top.

Gift Goodies

Food from your own kitchen is always appreciated during the holidays. Every family has its specialty. At our house we make "Aunt Reba's" cakes. No holiday is complete without this dessert and my sisters, my mother, my grandmother, and I all make a bunch of them to give as gifts.

Jams and jellies are favorites and it's fun to wrap them specially with colorful identifying gift tags. Place several jars in a basket to give as a gift. The gift tags are easy to make with heavy paper, fat markers (we used Uni Posca markers from Faber Castell, available in art stores), and scissors. The patterns are full size so you can trace and cut out as many as needed.

MATERIALS

A sheet of heavy white paper
(available in art stores)
A variety of colorful markers with
fat nibs

Red and green embroidery floss
Embroidery needle
Tracing paper
Ballpoint pen

DIRECTIONS

1. Trace the fruit shapes with a ballpoint pen.
2. Place the tracing face down on the heavy paper and rub over the back of the drawn lines with a pencil to transfer the design. To make more than one of each fruit shape, simply go over the outline with the pen and transfer by rubbing over the back once more. Repeat as many times as desired.
3. Use markers to color in each shape. Add details as indicated on the patterns.
4. Cut out each shape.
5. Cut a 12-inch length of red or green embroidery floss and thread the needle. Insert the needle at the top of each gift tag to attach the floss and tie around the neck of a jam jar.

Note: Consider cutting squares of checked or homespun fabric to decorate the top of each jar. Use pinking shears to cut each square and secure to the top with an elastic band before tying the tag around the neck.

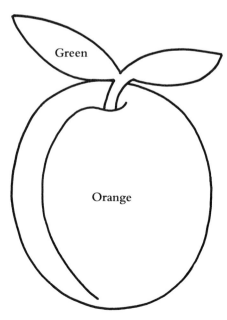

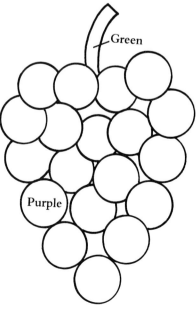

Green

Orange

Green

Purple

57

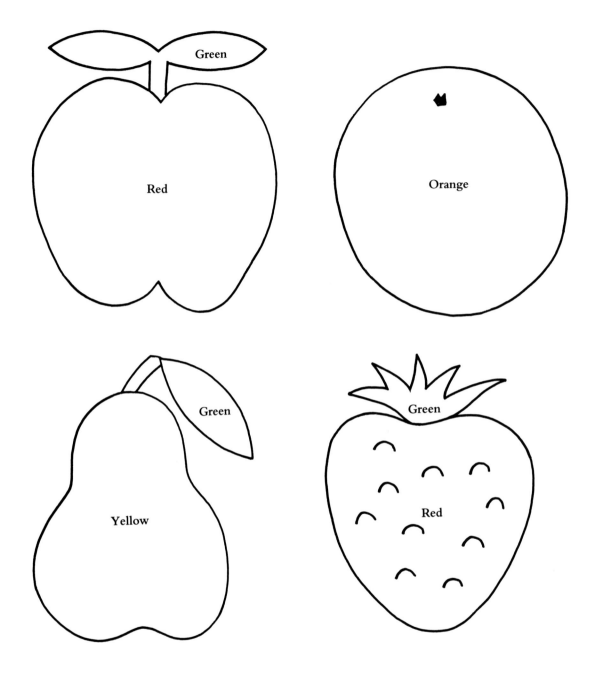

Pretty and Practical
Kitchen Set

Practical gifts don't have to look ordinary. Everyone needs new dishtowels and potholders from time to time and these are the things we hate to buy for ourselves. If you buy plain, inexpensive dishtowels you can decorate them with colorful appliqués. Then make a plain potholder and decorate it with a matching appliqué and give as gifts.

MATERIALS

For Dishtowels

2 white dishtowels
Small piece of red calico

Small piece of yellow calico
Small piece of solid green fabric

For Potholder

¼ yard white fabric
8 × 8-inch piece of thick quilt batting
Small piece of red calico

Scrap of green calico
1 yard green double-fold seam binding

For Dishtowels and Potholder

Tracing paper
Ballpoint pen
Heavy paper, such as manila folder
Fusible webbing (available in fabric stores)

Transfuse II (optional, available in fabric and craft stores)
Red, yellow, and green thread

DIRECTIONS

To Make Templates

Note: Use patterns from Gift Goodies, pages 57–58.
1. Refer to page 8. Using a ballpoint pen, trace each pattern piece. Place the tracings face down on heavy paper and rub over the back of the drawn lines with a pencil to transfer the designs.
2. Cut out all transferred pattern pieces.

To Prepare Fabric for Appliqué

1. Cut the fusible webbing to the same size as each fabric piece and place on the wrong side of the fabric. If you are not using Transfuse II, pin the fusible webbing to the back of each fabric piece.
2. If you are using Transfuse II (see page 7), place it over the webbing and press with a medium hot iron for five seconds. Peel away the Transfuse II. This process creates a fusible backing so that any fabric becomes iron-on for easy appliqué.

To Make Appliqués

1. For the dishtowels: Begin with the apple template and place on the wrong side of the red calico fabric. Trace the shape 3 times.
2. Using the pear template and the yellow fabric, repeat step 1.
3. Using the leaf pattern and the green fabric, repeat step 1.
4. For the potholder: Use the strawberry template and the red calico and repeat step 1. Repeat with the leaf template and green calico.
5. Cut out all pieces.

To Apply Appliqués

1. Find the center of the bottom edge of the dishtowel and position one red calico apple approximately 4 inches up from the edge.
2. Place the stem with leaves at the top of the apple. Fuse the appliqué to the dishtowel by pressing with a medium hot iron for 2 to 3 seconds.
3. With approximately 1 inch between appliqués, position a pear and stem on each side of the apple. Fuse to the background.
4. For the second towel: Arrange a pear in the center with an apple on each side.
5. Using corresponding color thread, zigzag-stitch around all raw edges of each appliqué, stem, and leaves.

To Make Potholder

1. From the white fabric cut 2 squares, each 8 × 8 inches.
2. Arrange both strawberries with stems in position on the front of 1 white square. Fuse with a medium hot iron as for the dishtowel appliqués.
3. Using red thread, zigzag-stitch around the edges of the strawberries. Use green to stitch around the stems.

To Finish Potholder

1. With wrong sides facing and raw edges aligned, pin the top, batting, and backing piece of fabric together.
2. Pin the seam binding all around the edges of the potholder. Stitch around as close to the open edge as possible.
3. Make a loop with the remaining piece of seam binding. Overlap the raw ends and stitch to the back of the top corner.

Here's what's cookin': Spicy In-
Recipe from: Ma
Preparation -
- D
2
1/2

Here's what's cookin': Lemon Mousse
Recipe from: Mama   serves 4
Delicious !!
1 can sweetened condensed milk
1/3 c. lemon or lime juice.
1/4 tsp salt
1 T. grated lime rind (use lemon
        rind if no lime)
1) Put cond. milk in bowl
2) Slowly add lemon ja while
        beating with whisk.
3) add grated rind + salt.
                        (over)

All through the House

Decorating for the holidays is quite special. For a whole month everything seems magical. There's so much to do and so many opportunities to make the things we love making at this time of year. A tree skirt, a welcoming banner, shadow appliqué pillows, card holders, and a pretty centerpiece for the holiday table are but a few of the things we've created for this chapter. Some of the decorations will make wonderful gifts, if you can part with them.

Schoolhouse Floorcloth

This stenciled floorcloth is as easy to do as coloring. Once the outline is created for each of the design elements you just fill in the color with a marker. If you make an error and color outside the lines, you can cover the mistake easily with the right color because we used opaque markers. The finished size of the floorcloth is 29 × 33 inches.

MATERIALS (all available in art stores)

Artist's canvas 35 × 39 inches
Cream-colored latex or acrylic
  paint for the background
Uni Posca markers from Faber
  Castell or acrylic paint—1 each
  of blue, red, white, and black

2-inch-wide sponge paint brush
Set of 2-inch-high stencil letters
Polyurethane (spray or regular)
White craft glue
Tools: ruler, tracing paper, and
  pencil

DIRECTIONS

1. Paint the entire canvas with cream color and set aside to dry.
2. Tape pieces of tracing paper together to create a piece same size as the canvas. On the tracing paper, make a grid of 1-inch squares to measure 29 × 33 inches.
3. Copy the dots in Figure 1 onto the tracing paper in the same positions.
4. Center the tracing paper on the canvas and transfer the dots by pushing your pencil through the tracing paper and making a mark on the canvas for each dot.
5. Refer to Figure 1 and connect the dots to create the design. You will have a border around the design with an excess of canvas all around for folding under, when finished, to create a neat edge.
6. Using the white marker, fill in all 26 blocks.
7. Outline each block with the blue marker and curve the inside corners to look like old-fashioned country blocks.
8. Beginning with the A stencil, center the letter on the first block in the left-hand corner and, using the blue marker, fill in the area. Repeat with each successive letter to create an alphabet border.
9. Using the red, black, and blue markers, fill in each area of the house with color as in photo.

To Finish

1. When the colors are dry, give the entire canvas a coat of polyurethane. Let dry thoroughly and recoat for further protection of the design.
2. Clip each corner at a 45-degree angle. Using a blunt instrument like a butter knife, score the outside line so the canvas will fold easily.
3. With face down, apply glue to the back of the 3 inches of folded canvas all around.
4. Fold all edges to the back and press down firmly. If necessary, weight the canvas down with heavy books until the glue dries.

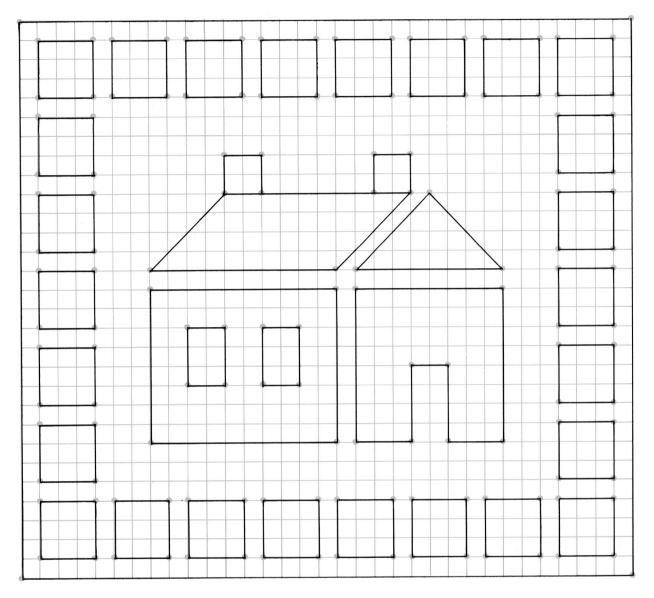

Figure 1. Create design by joining dots
　　　Each square equals 1 inch

Table Glamour

Dress up your table for the holidays with a stenciled table-cover and matching planter. Acrylic paint is used to apply the design, which is permanent and will not wash off the fabric, but will eventually wash off the ceramic.

The pretty red flowers with bright green leaves create a nice design for the holidays, but can be used all year long. The same design is used on the cloth as on the ceramic pot and you might find other objects on which to apply this design. For example, if you have a round table that needs refurbishing, consider repainting it and applying the stencil design directly to the tabletop.

The colors you choose for the stencil can match the fabric or wallpaper in your kitchen or dining room. This design looks good in pastels as well as in these bright colors.

The tablecover is 30 inches in diameter. It is meant to be used on a small table or placed in the center of a larger tablecloth. If you want to make a larger cloth, simply cut a circle of fabric to the desired size. All the materials for stenciling are available in art stores and some home centers.

MATERIALS

1 yard white fabric
1 package double-fold red bias binding
Tracing paper
Stencil paper
X-Acto craft knife

Stencil brush
Red and green acrylic paint (small tubes)
Masking tape
Planter

DIRECTIONS

To Make the Stencils

1. Trace the flowers as one stencil and the vine and leaves as another stencil.
2. Using a piece of stencil paper an inch or two larger all around than the design, tape each tracing over a piece of stencil paper.
3. Place these units on a cutting surface and, using a craft knife, cut through each traced design and the stencil paper.

To Make the Tablecloth

1. Cut a 32-inch length of string and tape one end to the center of the fabric.
2. Wrap the other end around a pencil and tape securely so you have a length of string 30 inches long. Holding the taped end of the string to the center of the cloth, pull the pencil until the string is taut and draw a circle all around. Cut out.
3. To finish the edges, pin and stitch the red bias binding all around the circle.

To Stencil Tablecloth

1. Fold the fabric in half and then in half again so you are working with a quarter of the tablecloth.
2. Place the fabric on a hard, flat surface and tape to hold taut. Measure 3 inches in from the edge and center the flower stencil on the fabric. Tape in position on the cloth as shown in Figure 1. Temporarily mask out the stems by placing pieces of tape over these areas.
3. Squirt a small amount of red paint onto a dish or paper plate. (It will wash off the dish with hot water).
4. Using a dry stencil brush, lightly dip the end into the paint. Tap the brush up and down on newspaper to blot, then onto the fabric through the cutout flower section only. Do not brush the paint on, but rather apply it in a firm up-and-down motion. To darken the color or create shading, go over the same area several times, always using a nearly dry brush.
5. The paint will dry quickly and you will then turn the fabric over and repeat the process on each quarter section of the tablecloth.
6. When all the red flowers have been stenciled, clean the brush thoroughly and let it dry before starting with the green color.
7. Next, remove the tape from the green stem cutout areas and position the stencil, using the flowers as a guide. Tape the stencil in position and mask the flowers out with pieces of tape. Apply the green paint to the stem areas under each flower.
8. Position the curving vine and leaves between each of the flower designs and tape to the fabric. Using green paint, stencil these areas as before.

To Finish

When the paint is completely dry, place the tablecloth face down on an ironing board covered with a scrap piece of fabric. Press the back of the cloth with a medium hot iron to set the paint. The stenciled fabric can now be washed in warm or cold (not hot) water without losing the design.

To Stencil Planter

It's a bit trickier to stencil on a curved surface. The process, however, is the same. You'll need only one design on the front, or two if you want the design to wrap around the planter. Tape the cutout stencil in position and apply the paint as you did onto the cloth. It will take a little longer to dry, but the paint should not be applied too heavily. It is best to tap many light coats over the surface to fill in the color. We added a trim of green paint around the top of the planter.

This design can be used to stencil on a wicker basket, wooden container, or glass. When stenciling on wicker, the design will be more open because the surface isn't smooth, but it can still be an interesting project.

If you stencil this design on a painted wooden tabletop, for example, apply a coat of polyurethane or varnish over all when finished to preserve the design and painted finish.

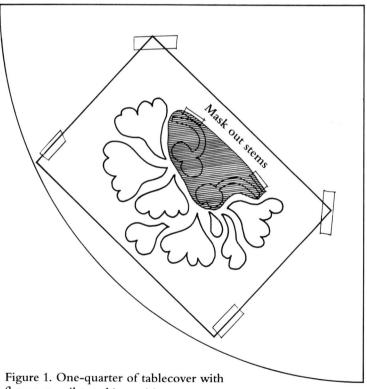

Figure 1. One-quarter of tablecover with flower stencil taped in position

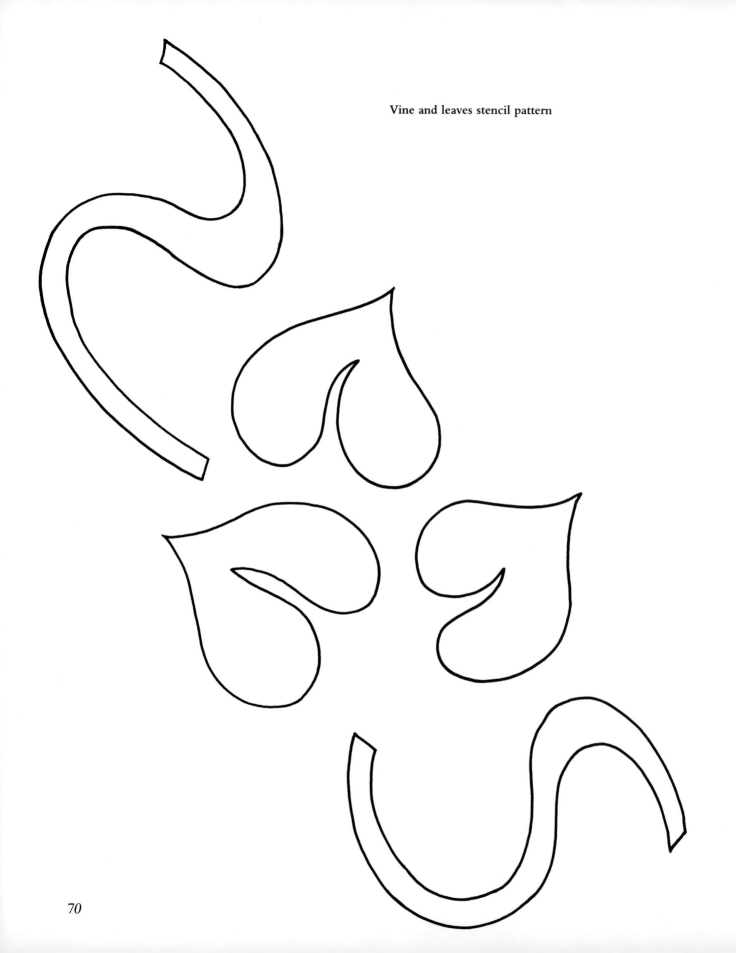

Vine and leaves stencil pattern

70

Flower stencil pattern

Tulip Runner

Decorate any table with a holiday runner. This one is appliquéd with country tulips and leaves made from calicos and solids. The center square is left plain for holding a vase of flowers or a centerpiece. Arrange a Christmas scene with fresh greens, clove-studded fruit, ornaments, candles, and little holiday decorations. The finished runner is 13 × 37 inches and will fit nicely on a dining table, sideboard, or hallway table.

MATERIALS

½ yard white fabric
½ yard green fabric
½ yard red calico
Small piece of light green fabric
13 × 37-inch piece of thin quilt
  batting
Fusible webbing (available in
  fabric stores)

Transfuse II (optional, available in
  fabric and craft stores)
Tracing paper
Heavy paper, such as manila
  folder

DIRECTIONS

Note: Use ¼-inch seam allowance when joining fabrics.

Cut the following:

From green:
  2 squares, each 12½ × 12½ inches
From white:
  1 square 12½ × 12½ inches
From red calico:
  1 piece 13½ × 37½ inches for backing
  Borders
    2 strips, each 1 × 37½ inches (top and bottom)
    2 strips, each 1 × 12½ inches (sides)

To Make Runner

1. With right sides facing and raw edges aligned, stitch a green square to the white square along one side edge. Open seams and press.
2. Join the remaining green square to the opposite side of the white square to form a row of 3 squares. Open seams and press.
3. With right sides facing and raw edges aligned, stitch a red calico 1 × 12½ inch strip to each side edge of the runner. Open seams and press.
4. Next, join the 1 × 37½-inch red calico strips to the top and bottom edges of the runner in the same way. Open seams and press.
5. Set backing fabric aside for finishing step.

To Make Templates

1. Refer to page 8. Trace the tulip, leaf, and stem patterns on page 75 with a pencil.
2. Place the tracings face down on heavy paper and rub over the back of the traced lines with a pencil to transfer.
3. Cut out all pieces.

To Make Appliqués

1. Begin by cutting the fusible webbing same size as the remaining red calico and light green fabrics. If you are not using Transfuse II, pin the fusible webbing to the back of each fabric piece.
2. If you are using Transfuse II (see page 7), place the fusible webbing on the wrong side of the fabric and the Transfuse II on top of it. Press with a medium hot iron for 5 seconds, then peel off the Transfuse II.
3. Place the tulip template on the red calico and trace around the outline. Make 8. Repeat with the leaf template on the light green fabric. Make 24. Repeat with the stem template on light green fabric. Make 4.
4. Cut out all elements.
5. Trace the pattern from page 75. This is one-half of the runner design. Turn the tracing as indicated in pattern diagram and trace again so you have a tracing of the entire design.
6. Center the tracing on a green square and using this as a placement guide, position each tulip, stem, and leaf under the tracing.
7. Remove the tracing paper and fuse all pieces to the background with a medium hot iron. If you have not used fusible webbing or Transfuse II, simply pin each appliqué in position on the fabric. Repeat steps 6 and 7 on the remaining green square.
8. Using thread color to match each appliqué, zigzag-stitch around all edges.

To Finish

1. Pin the top, quilt batting, and backing fabric together.
2. Stitch along the seam line where the red calico border meets the top of the runner.
3. Turn the raw edges of the top and backing to the inside ¼ inch and press.
4. Slip-stitch or machine-stitch around as close to edge as possible.

Tulip pattern for runner

Tulip Placemats

Make country placemats for yourself or to give as a gift. They're easy to make with the full-size tulip appliqués. These were designed to match the table runner (see page 72) and together they make a special gift or holiday decoration for informal meals. The directions are for making four placemats, each 12 × 16 inches.

MATERIALS

¼ yard light green fabric
¾ yard white fabric
1 yard red calico
24 × 32-inch piece of thin quilt batting
Fusible webbing (available in fabric stores)

Transfuse II (optional, available in fabric and craft stores)
Tracing paper
Heavy paper, such as a manila folder

DIRECTIONS

Note: Use ¼-inch seam allowance for joining all fabrics.

Cut the following:

From green:
 4 rectangles, each 4½ × 11½ inches
From white:
 4 pieces, each 11½ × 11½ inches
From red calico:
 4 pieces, each 12½ × 16½ inches for backing
 Borders
  8 strips, each 1 × 16½ inches (top and bottom)
  8 strips, each 1 × 12½ inches (sides)
From quilt batting:
 4 pieces, each 12 × 16 inches

To Make Placemats

1. With right sides facing and raw edges aligned, stitch the left side of a white square to the right long edge of a green rectangle.
2. Open seams and press.
3. With right sides facing and raw edges aligned, stitch a red calico strip 1 × 12½ inches to each side edge of the placemat. Open seams and press.

4. Next, stitch a 1 × 16½-inch red calico strip to the top and bottom edges of the placemat in the same way. Open seams and press.

To Make Templates and Prepare Appliqués

See pages 73–74 for Tulip Runner.

To Finish

1. Trace the tulip pattern on page 78, which is half the design.
2. Turn the tracing around and trace the other half to create a full tracing of the design.
3. Use the tracing as a guide and center it over the green strip of the placemat.

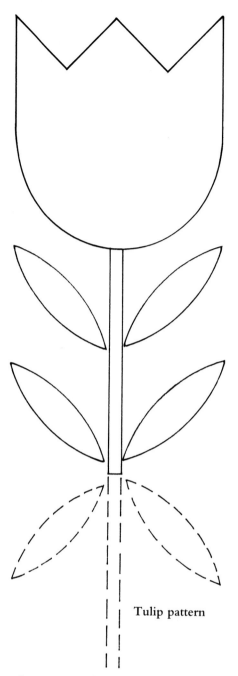

Tulip pattern

Begin by positioning the stem under the tracing. Add a tulip at each end and then 8 leaves as indicated on your tracing.

4. Remove the tracing paper and fuse each appliqué to the placemat with a medium hot iron. If you have not used fusible webbing or Transfuse II, pin each appliqué in position on the fabric.

5. Using a thread color to match each design element, zigzag-stitch around the raw edges.

6. Pin the top, quilt batting, and backing together.

7. Machine-stitch along the seam line around the border.

8. Turn the raw edges of the top and backing to the inside ¼ inch and press. Slip-stitch or machine-stitch around as close to the edge as possible.

Shadow Appliqué Pillows

Shadow appliqué is a variation on traditional appliqué. It is interesting and easier to create. The process of fusing colorful fabrics to the background eliminates the need to turn under the fabric edges. A thin piece of organza is then placed over the appliqué and the background fabric. The colors of the appliqué are toned down for a subtle effect. Hand-quilting around the appliqué makes the design stand out and holds all layers of fabric together. The pillows shown here are 16 × 16 inches.

MATERIALS (for 2 pillows)

½ yard red calico
½ yard green calico
½ yard white fabric
½ yard organza (sheer overlay fabric)
½ yard thin quilt batting
2 pillow forms, each 16 × 16 inches, or stuffing
2 zippers, each 14 inches (optional)

4 yards ¼-inch cording
Fusible webbing (available in fabric stores)
Transfuse II (optional, available in fabric and craft stores)
Tracing paper
Heavy paper, such as manila folder

DIRECTIONS

Note: Use ¼-inch seam allowance for all sewing.

Cut the following:

From red calico:
   2 squares, each 16½ × 16½ inches for backing
From green calico:
   4 strips, each ½ × 33 inches, for the piping
From white:
   2 squares, each 16½ × 16½ inches
From organza:
   2 squares, each 17 × 17 inches
From quilt batting:
   2 squares, each 16 × 16 inches

Pillows 1 and 2

1. Trace the stem and leaf pattern pieces on page 84 and transfer to the heavy paper to make templates (see page 8).

2. Cut fusible webbing same size as the remaining rose and green calico fabrics and place on the wrong side of the fabric pieces. If you are not using Transfuse II, pin the fusible webbing to the back of each fabric piece.

3. If you are using Transfuse II (see page 7), place it over the fusible webbing and press with a medium hot iron for 5 seconds. Peel away Transfuse II.

Pillow 1

1. Place the stem template on the green calico and draw around the pattern. Make 4. Using the green calico and the larger leaf template, make 4. Using green and small leaf template, make 16. Using red calico and large leaf template, make 4. Using red calico and small leaf template, make 8.

2. Cut out all fabric pieces. If you haven't used Transfuse II to make iron-on fabric, simply cut the shapes from both the fabric and the fusible webbing. (The fusible webbing will be placed between the fabric background and the fabric appliqué, then fused to the background with a hot iron.)

3. Trace the pattern for Pillow 1 as shown in Figure 1. This is one-quarter of the design. Turn the tracing and continue to trace the design 3 more times to create the entire design. Use this tracing as a placement guide for all appliqué.

4. Center the tracing on a white square of fabric and arrange each pattern piece in position under the tracing. Remove tracing paper and iron down each appliqué piece.

Pillow 2

1. Place the stem template on the green calico and draw around the outline. Make 4. Using the green calico, make 8 small leaves and 8 large leaves in the same way. Using the red calico, make 4 small leaves and 4 large leaves.

2. Cut out all pieces.

3. Trace the pattern for Pillow 2 as shown in Figure 2, which is one-quarter of the design. Turn the paper and trace 3 more times as you did for Pillow 1 to complete the design.

4. Using this as an overlay, arrange all appliqué pieces on a white square. Remove tracing and iron pieces in place.

5. Trace the quilting pattern (Figure 3) and transfer to the center of the white fabric (see page 8).

To Complete Shadow Appliqué

1. Place one organza square over each pillow top and pin each to a square of quilt batting. Baste all 3 layers of fabric loosely together around the edges.

2. Using small running stitch (see page 11), quilt along the outside edge of

Figure 1. Pattern for Pillow 1

Figure 2. Pattern for Pillow 2

83

each appliqué piece through all layers of fabric. For added interest, quilt ¼ inch outside the first quilting stitches (see page 9).

3. On Pillow 2 only, follow the quilt lines on the center design.

To Make Piping

1. With right sides facing and raw edges aligned, stitch 2 green calico strips together along the short ends.

2. Place the cording in the center of the wrong side of the fabric strip and fold the strip so the long raw edges meet, encasing the cording between.

3. Using a zipper foot on your machine, stitch the fabric together as close to the cording as possible.

4. With right sides facing and raw edges aligned, pin the piping around the front of the pillow top. Clip into the seam allowance at the corners so the piping will turn neatly at these points.

5. Using the piping stitches as a guide, stitch the piping to the pillow top.

To Finish Both Pillows

1. With right sides facing and raw edges aligned, pin the backing to the front of the pillow with the piping between.

2. Stitch around 3 sides and 4 corners, leaving last side open for turning.

3. Clip the corners and turn right side out. Insert zipper if desired or turn raw edges to inside and press.

4. Insert pillow form or stuffing and slip-stitch opening closed.

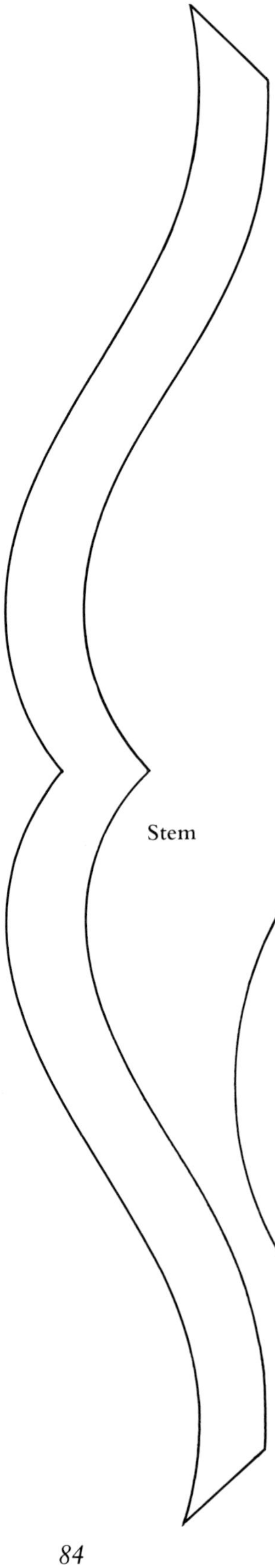

Stem

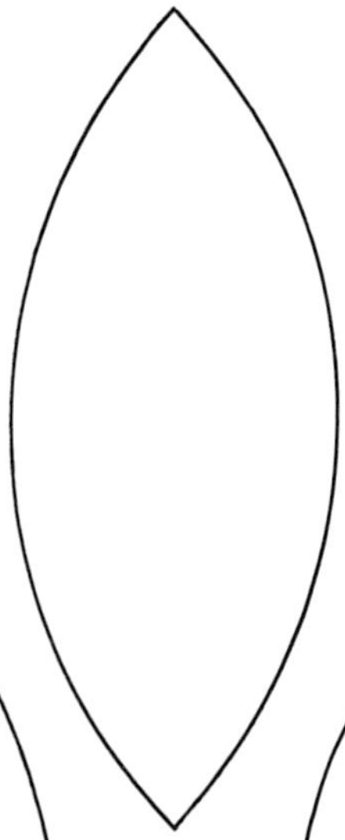

Large leaf

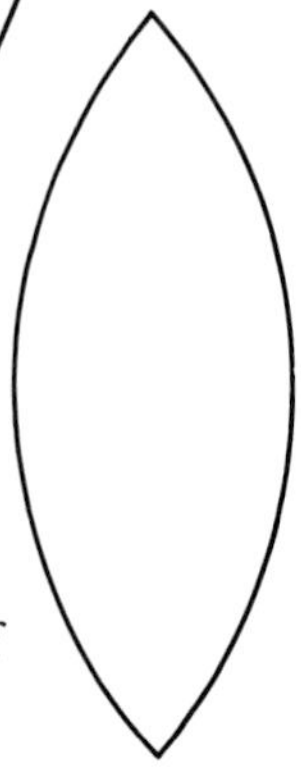

Small leaf

Figure 3. Quilting pattern for center of Pillow 2

Four Seasons Wallhanging

Make a quilted wallhanging with a country scene representing the four seasons. This is a good way to use up all the scraps in your sewing basket. Hang the finished wallhanging in a child's room, kitchen, or hallway. It can hang as is or you might consider stretching and framing it when finished. The finished size is 21 × 23 inches.

MATERIALS

Assorted scraps of calicos, prints (including a pin dot for winter scene), and solid fabrics
¼ yard light blue fabric
¼ yard blue-and-white striped fabric
¾ yard royal blue fabric
21 × 23 inch piece of thin quilt batting

Fusible webbing (available in fabric stores)
Transfuse II (optional, available in fabric and craft stores)
Black embroidery floss
Embroidery needle
Tracing paper
Velcro tabs for hanging

DIRECTIONS

Note: Measurements for all fabric strips and backing for the quilt include ¼-inch seam allowance. No seam allowance is needed for appliqué pieces. Cut pattern pieces on the given lines. All are shown full size.

Cut the following:

From light blue:
    3 pieces, each 8 × 9 inches
From blue-and-white stripes:
    1 piece 8 × 9 inches
From royal blue:
    1 piece 21½ × 23½ inches for backing
    2 strips 2½ × 12½ inches
    Borders
        3 strips, each 2½ × 19½ inches (top, middle, and bottom)
        2 strips, each 2½ × 21½ inches (sides)

Preparing to Appliqué

1. Begin by deciding which scrap fabric pieces will be used for each scene on the wallhanging. For example, you will need the same fabric for all 4 houses since these won't change with the seasons. You will use white for

the clouds in each scene, although their shapes will be different. You might use a brown calico for the trunk of the tree in 3 scenes, but use black for the bare tree of winter. There will be autumn colors on the ground in the fall and brighter colors used for the summer scene. The colors of the sky will vary as well, with the winter sky slightly gray rather than blue.

2. Once you've determined the fabrics for each scene, cut pieces of fusible webbing to the size of the fabric scraps to be used.

3. To make each piece iron-on and therefore easy to handle and apply, place the fusible webbing on the wrong side of the fabric and Transfuse II (see page 7) on top of it. Press with a medium hot iron for 5 seconds. Peel away the Transfuse II and the fabric is now ready for cutting into shapes. If you do not use Transfuse II, pin the fusible webbing to the back of each fabric piece.

To Make Appliqués

1. Trace each element for each scene.
2. Using the photograph of the finished project as a guide, select fabrics for each element.
3. Pin each pattern piece to the chosen fabric and cut out.
4. Trace each complete scene to use as an overlay for correct placement.

To Create a Scene

1. For the winter scene use the striped fabric and arrange the cutout pieces according to the number sequence in Figure 1.
2. Place the tracing over the background to be sure all pieces are in place.
3. Remove tracing and fuse each piece to the background with a medium hot iron.
4. Using the blue fabric, continue with spring (Figure 2), summer (Figure 3), and fall (Figure 4) in this way.
5. Using 3 strands of black embroidery floss add details such as the eyes, mouth, and buttons to the snowman with little knots. Use a running stitch (see page 11) to create the rope connecting the tire swing to the tree in the summer scene.

To Join Scenes

1. Refer to Figure 5. With right sides facing and raw edges aligned, stitch a 2½ × 12½-inch royal blue strip along the right side edge of the winter scene.
2. Open seams and press.
3. Next, join the spring scene to the right side edge of the blue strip in the same way. You now have a row of 2 scenes divided by a blue strip.
4. With right sides facing and raw edges aligned, join another blue strip of the same size to the right side edge of the summer scene. Open seams and press.
5. Next, join fall to the right side edge of the blue strip to create the bottom row of summer and fall scenes.
6. Open seams and press.

To Join Rows

1. With right sides facing and raw edges aligned, stitch a 2½ × 19½-inch royal blue strip to the top edge of the top row (winter/spring).
2. Open seams and press.
3. Next, join another royal blue strip of the same size to the bottom edge of this top row. Open seams and press.
4. With right sides facing and raw edges aligned, stitch the summer/fall row to the bottom edge of the divider strip. Open seams and press.
5. With right sides facing and raw edges aligned, stitch the remaining royal blue strip of the same size to the bottom edge of the row. Open seams and press.

To Add Borders

1. With right sides facing and raw edges aligned, stitch a 2½ × 21½-inch royal blue strip to each side of the wallhanging.
2. Open seams and press.

To Finish

1. With right sides facing and raw edges aligned, place the top and backing together.
2. Next, place the quilt batting on top of the fabric and pin all 3 layers together.
3. Machine-stitch around 3 sides and 4 corners, leaving an opening for turning.
4. Trim the seam allowance, clip corners, and turn right side out.
5. Turn the raw edges to the inside ¼ inch and press. Slip-stitch opening closed.

To Hang

Since this project is quite light you can easily hang it with Velcro tabs attached at the back of each corner. Attach corresponding tabs in position on the wall and simply press the wallhanging in place.

Figure 1. Winter

Numbers indicate order in which to attach pieces

89

Figure 2. Spring

Numbers indicate order in which to attach pieces

90

Figure 3. Summer

Numbers indicate order in which to attach pieces

Figure 4. Fall

Numbers indicate order in which to attach pieces

Marching Soldier Banner

Greet guests with a simple, no-sew banner of marching soldiers. Each soldier holds a flag bearing a letter. Together they say "NOEL" in bold, bright letters. We used iron-on felt for the appliqué pieces. If you can't find this in your local fabric or craft store, use fusible webbing to adhere the felt pieces to the background or glue each piece. Only the bias binding around the edges is stitched. The finished project is 16 × 23 inches.

MATERIALS

½ yard plain white felt for background

Small piece of white fusible felt for the letters

¼ yard fusible red felt

Small piece of fusible felt in each of the following colors: navy blue, black, yellow, pink, green, and rose (or use fusible webbing or glue with plain felt)

2¼ yards double-fold green bias binding

Fusible webbing (available in fabric stores) or white craft glue if plain felt is used

Tracing paper

Velcro tabs or plastic curtain rings for hanging

DIRECTIONS

Note: All appliqué pieces are given full size. No seam allowance is needed.

Cut the following:

From plain white felt:
   1 piece 16 × 23 inches for the banner
From fusible red felt:
   4 pieces, each 3½ × 3¾ inches for the flags

To Prepare

1. Trace one of each pattern piece for standing soldier in Figure 1.
2. Trace each pattern piece for the marching soldiers in Figure 2 four times.
3. Trace one of each letter in Figure 3.
4. Pin the traced patterns to felt of the colors indicated on the pattern pieces and cut out.

To Make Soldiers

1. Begin by positioning the standing soldier so his left arm is placed 2 inches in from the left side of the white background and his feet are 2 inches up from the bottom edge.
2. Refer to Figure 1 and arrange all the pieces as indicated.
3. Place a thin piece of scrap fabric over the fusible felt pieces or plain felt with fusible webbing and, using a medium hot iron, press for 5 seconds to fuse the felt pieces to the background. Or glue each piece in position if you have used plain felt.
4. Beginning 2 inches up from the bottom edge, arrange all the pieces to create the 4 marching soldiers. There should be 3 inches between the heels of each soldier's standing leg.
5. Repeat step 3.

To Make Flags

1. From black felt, cut 4 thin strips, each 9½ inches long, for the flag poles.
2. Arrange each pole so that it runs through the center of the outstretched

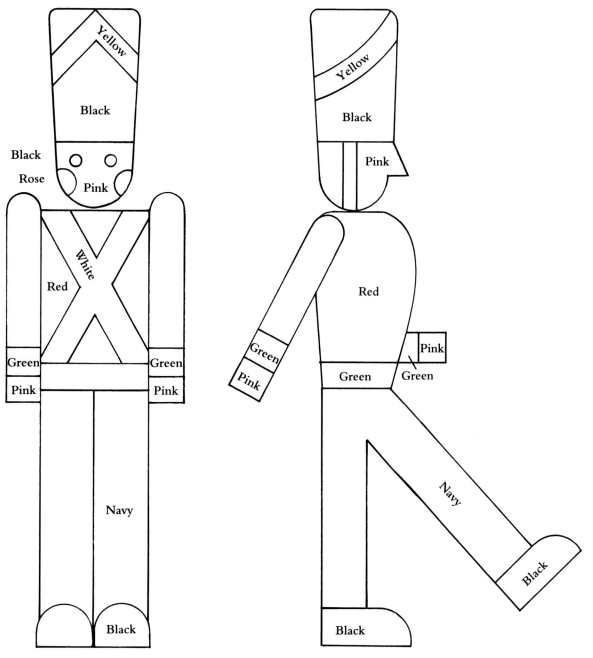

Figure 1. Standing soldier

Figure 2. Marching soldier

Figure 3. Letter Patterns

hand and the bottom of the pole touches the outstretched leg of each march-ing soldier.

3. Place a scrap piece of fabric over each pole and, using a medium hot iron, press for 5 seconds. If you have not used fusible felt or fusible webbing, glue the poles.

4. Next, arrange the red felt squares so each is flush with the top edge of each pole as shown in the photograph.

5. Repeat step 3.

6. Center each letter on a red flag and repeat step 3 as before.

To Finish

1. Pin the green bias binding around the outside edge of the felt banner.

2. Machine-stitch all around.

3. There are two ways to hang the banner. One is to use Velcro tabs on the back of each top corner and in the center of the top edge. Attach cor-responding tabs to the wall and press in position. Or attach plastic curtain rings to the back at each top corner and hang on small hooks.

Christmas Quilt and Pillow

A quilt and matching pillow made for the holidays is the perfect gift for a special person on your list. The finished quilt is 48 × 60 inches, which is perfect for a lap throw or a wallhanging. The patchwork and quilting were stitched by Corrinne Allesandrello.

Quilt

MATERIALS (all fabric is 45 inches wide)

¼ yard dark red calico
1½ yards bright red calico
1¾ yards dark green calico
3 yards black or navy calico
   (includes backing)

Traditional quilt batting, 48 × 60 inches
Heavy paper, such as manila folder
Tracing paper

DIRECTIONS

Note: All measurements include ¼-inch seam allowance.
1. Begin by tracing each of the pattern pieces for templates 1 and 2.
2. Refer to page 8 for making templates.

Cut the following:

From dark red calico:
   12 squares, each 4½ × 4½ inches
From bright red calico:
   Borders
      2 strips, each 2½ × 36½ inches (top and bottom)
      2 strips, each 2½ × 52½ inches (sides)
   96 pieces from template 1
From dark green calico:
   Borders
      2 strips, each 4½ × 40½ inches (top and bottom)
      2 strips, each 4½ × 60½ inches (sides)
   24 squares, each 4½ × 4½ inches
   24 pieces from template 2
From black or navy calico:
   2 pieces, each 31 × 49 inches for backing
   24 squares, each 4½ × 4½ inches
   24 pieces from template 2

Patterns for templates

Block A

1. Refer to Figure 1. With right sides facing and raw edges aligned, stitch the diagonal side of a red template 1 piece to each side of a black calico template 2 piece to make a square. This is Unit 1. Make 4.
2. Open seams and press.

To Make Rows

1. With right sides facing and raw edges aligned, stitch a green calico square to Unit 1 along one side edge. Open seams and press.
2. Refer to Figure 2. Stitch another green calico square to the opposite side of Unit 1 to make Row 1 of Block A.
3. With right sides facing and raw edges aligned, stitch Unit 1 to a dark red calico square along one side edge. Open seams and press.

4. Refer to Figure 2. Stitch another Unit 1 to the opposite side of the dark red calico square to make Row 2 of Block A.

5. Repeat steps 1 and 2 to make Row 3 of Block A.

To Join Rows

1. Refer to Figure 3. With right sides facing and raw edges aligned, stitch Row 1 and Row 2 together along the bottom edge. Open seams and press.

2. Next, with right sides facing and raw edges aligned, stitch Row 2 to Row 3 in the same way.

3. Make 6 of Block A in this way.

Block B

This block is made as you made Block A, with different colors. Use the green calico template 2 pieces in place of the black calico template 2 pieces in Unit 1 and black calico squares in place of green calico squares.

To Make Rows

1. Row 1: With right sides together and raw edges aligned, stitch Block A to Block B along the right side edge. Open seams and press.

2. Join another Block A to Block B in the same way to make a row of 3 blocks.

3. Row 2: With right sides facing and raw edges aligned, stitch Block B to Block A. Open seams and press.

4. Next, join another Block B to Block A in the same way.

5. Row 3: Repeat steps 1 and 2.

6. Row 4: Repeat steps 3 and 4.

To Join Rows

1. Refer to Figure 3. With right sides facing and raw edges aligned, stitch Row 1 to Row 2 along the bottom edge. Open seams and press.

2. Continue to join all 4 rows in this way.

To Add Borders

1. Refer to Figure 4. With right sides facing and raw edges aligned, join one bright red calico 2½ × 36½-inch strip to the top edge of the quilt. Open seams and press.

2. Repeat on the bottom edge.

3. With right sides facing and raw edges aligned, join the red calico side border strips in the same way.

4. With right sides facing and raw edges aligned, stitch a green calico 4½ × 40½-inch strip to the top edge of the quilt. Open seams and press.

5. Repeat on the bottom edge.

6. Next, stitch the remaining green calico strips to the sides of the quilt top in the same way. Open seams and press.

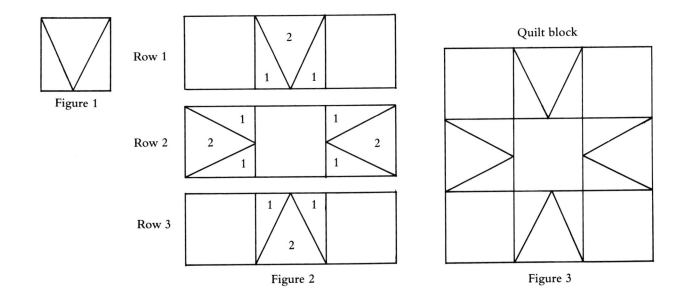

Figure 1

Row 1

Row 2

Row 3

Figure 2

Quilt block

Figure 3

To Quilt

1. With right sides facing and raw edges aligned, stitch the 2 backing pieces together to make a piece 49 × 62 inches.

2. Center the quilt batting on the wrong side of the backing and place the quilt top over the batting. Pin all 3 layers of fabric together. You will have extra backing fabric all around.

3. Beginning at the center of the quilt top, take long loose basting stitches in a starburst pattern so there are approximately 6 inches between the lines.

4. To hand-quilt (see page 9): Take small running stitches along ¼ inch on each side of all seam lines. *Do not stitch into the seam allowance all around.*

5. To machine-quilt (see page 9): Set the stitches to approximately 8 stitches per inch. Beginning at the center of the quilt top and working outward, machine-stitch along the seam lines of the patchwork, through all 3 layers of fabric. *Do not stitch into the seam allowance all around the quilt.*

6. Remove pins and basting stitches.

To Finish

1. Trim the batting ½ inch smaller than the quilt top all around.

2. Trim the backing to same size as quilt top all around.

3. Turn the raw edges of the quilt top ¼ inch to the inside and press. Turn raw edges of the backing ¼ inch to the inside and press. Pin together all around.

4. Machine- or slip-stitch opening closed all around outside edge of the quilt.

Figure 4. Christmas Quilt assembly

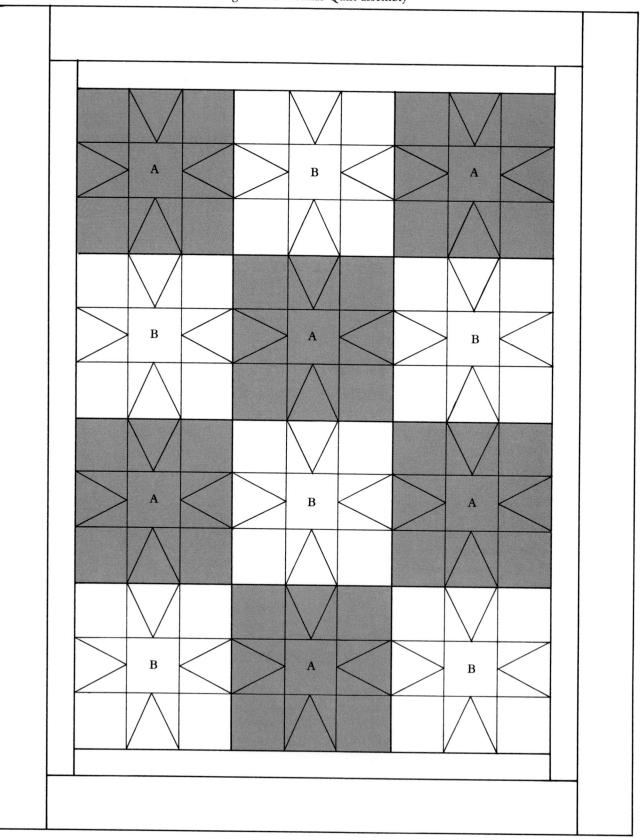

Star Pillow

The finished size of the pillow is 18 × 18 inches. The sizes of the patchwork pieces are the same as the quilt, and all measurements include ¼-inch seam allowance.

MATERIALS

Small piece of dark red calico
Small piece of dark green calico
¼ yard black or navy calico
¾ yard bright red calico
2 yards red piping
Thin quilt batting, 19 × 19 inches

18-inch pillow form or stuffing
16-inch zipper (optional)
Heavy paper, such as manila
   folder
Tracing paper

DIRECTIONS

To Make Template

1. Begin by tracing each of the pattern pieces for templates 1 and 2.
2. Refer to page 8 to make templates.

Cut the following:

From dark red calico:
   1 square 4½ × 4½ inches
From dark green calico:
   4 squares, each 4½ × 4½ inches
From black or navy calico:
   Borders
      2 strips, each 2½ × 14½ inches (top and bottom)
      2 strips, each 2½ × 18½ inches (sides)
   4 pieces from template 2
From bright red calico:
   Borders
      2 strips, each 1½ × 12½ inches (top and bottom)
      2 strips, each 1½ × 14½ inches (sides)
   1 square 18½ × 18½ inches for backing
   8 pieces from template 1

To Make a Square

1. Refer to Figure 1. With right sides facing and raw edges aligned, stitch a bright red calico template 1 to each diagonal side of a black calico template 2 piece.
2. Open seams and press. Make 4 pieced squares in this way.

To Make Rows

1. Refer to Figure 2. With right sides facing and raw edges aligned, stitch a green calico square to the left side edge of a pieced square as shown. Open seams and press.
2. Next, stitch a green calico square to the right side edge of the pieced square to complete Row 1 of the pillow top. Open seams and press.
3. Row 2: With right sides facing and raw edges aligned, stitch a pieced square to the left side edge of the dark red calico square as shown. Open seams and press.
4. Complete Row 2 by joining a pieced square to the right side edge of the center square as shown. Open seams and press.
5. Repeat steps 1 and 2 for Row 3.

To Join Rows

1. With right sides facing and raw edges aligned, stitch Row 1 and Row 2 together along the bottom edge. Open seams and press.
2. Join Row 2 and Row 3 in the same way to complete the pillow top as shown in Figure 3.

To Add Borders

1. Refer to Figure 5. With right sides facing and raw edges aligned, stitch a red 1½ × 12½-inch strip to the top edge of the pillow top. Open seams and press.
2. Repeat on the bottom edge.

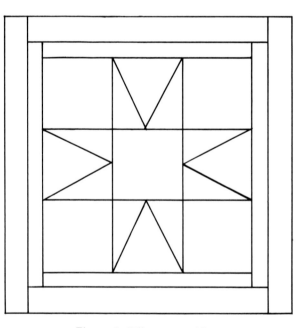

Figure 5. Pillow assembly

3. With right sides facing and raw edges aligned, stitch a bright red 1½ × 14½-inch strip to one side edge of the pillow top. Open seams and press.

4. Repeat with the remaining bright red side strip.

5. With right sides facing and raw edges aligned, stitch a black or navy calico 2½ × 14½-inch strip to the top edge of the pillow top. Open seams and press.

6. Repeat on bottom edge.

7. With right sides facing and raw edges aligned, stitch a black or navy calico 2½ × 18½-inch strip to one side edge. Open seams and press.

8. Repeat with remaining side strip to complete the patchwork pillow top.

To Quilt

1. Center the pillow top over the quilt batting square so there is an equal amount of extra batting all around and pin together.

2. Starting at the center and working outward in a sunburst pattern, baste the fabric together in long loose stitches.

3. To hand-quilt (see page 9): Using red, black, or green thread, take small running stitches ¼ inch on each side of all seam lines. *Do not stitch into the seam allowance all around.*

4. To machine-quilt (see page 9): With a stitch setting at approximately 8 stitches to the inch, machine-stitch along all seam lines. *Do not stitch into seam allowance all around.*

5. When all quilting is complete, remove basting stitches.

6. Trim batting to same size as quilted top.

To Finish

1. With raw edges aligned, pin the piping all around the front of the pillow top. Clip into seam allowance of the piping at each corner in order to turn easily.

2. Using a zipper foot on your machine, stitch around as close to the piping as possible.

3. With right sides facing and raw edges aligned, pin the backing to the top of the pillow with the piping between. Using the piping stitches as a guide, stitch around 3 sides and 4 corners, leaving an opening for turning.

4. Trim seam allowance and clip corners. Turn right side out and press.

5. Turn open edges to inside ¼ inch and press. If desired, stitch zipper in place according to package directions.

6. Insert pillow form or stuff with filling. If no zipper has been added, slip-stitch opening closed.

Snowman Cardholder

When season's greetings cards pile up, we usually line them on a windowsill, tape them around a door, arrange them on a table, or hang them from ribbons. These are all nice ways to enjoy the holiday cards, but they take up lots of room and tend to get in the way. A decorative card holder is the perfect solution. Enjoy receiving each card, then put it in the holder. As each new card arrives it is placed in the pocket on top of the others. The cards can be removed easily whenever you want to look at all of them together. After the holidays pack away the cardholder with the cards intact. The finished size is 8½ × 14½ inches, and the iron-on felt appliqués make this practically a no-sew project.

MATERIALS

¼ yard blue pin dot fabric

Small piece of fusible felt in each of the following colors: red, green, black, brown, and pink (or use fusible webbing with plain felt)

Piece of fusible white felt, 8½ × 12 inches

Piece of plain red felt, 5 × 8½ inches

Piece of red gingham, calico, or ribbon for trim, 2½ × 9 inches

Fusible webbing (available in fabric stores) if plain felt is used

Black embroidery floss (for snowman's mouth)

Tracing paper

2 small plastic curtain rings for hanging

DIRECTIONS

Note: All felt pattern pieces are shown full size; no seam allowance is needed.

1. From the pin dot fabric, cut a piece 9 × 15 inches for the background (includes ¼-inch seam allowance).

2. Turn the raw edges to the back ¼ inch and press. Turn under another ¼ inch, press, and machine-stitch all around to finish edges.

3. From the white felt, cut a piece 7 × 8½ inches.

4. Trace all pattern pieces and pin to fusible felt of the color indicated on each pattern. Cut out all pattern pieces. A paper punch is handy for cutting out circles for the snowman's eyes and nose. If you are using plain felt rather than iron-on felt, pin each pattern piece to the felt and then to the fusible webbing before cutting out each pattern piece.

To Assemble

1. Refer to Figure 1. The numbers indicate the order in which you should place the pieces. Put the large green tree on the pin dot background approximately 1 inch down from the top edge and 1 inch in from the left edge to the first branch. Cover the felt with a piece of fabric to protect it and press with a medium hot iron for 5 seconds.
2. Position the smaller tree approximately 1½ inches down from the top and 1 inch in from the right side edge. Press to fuse.
3. Next, position all the pieces on the snowman as indicated in Figure 1.
4. Fuse with a medium hot iron as before.
5. Referring to the diagram, center the snowman 2 inches down from the top edge and fuse to the background as before.
6. Add the top hat and shovel pieces.
7. Place the 7 × 8½-inch white felt piece across the trunk of the trees so it abuts the bottom edge of the snowman and aligns with the side edges of the background. Fuse in place.

To Make Pocket

1. Fold the raw edges of the gingham, ribbon, or calico trim fabric to the back ¼ inch and press.
2. Pin this strip to the top 2 inches of the plain red fabric piece and stitch across the top and bottom of the trim edges.
3. With bottom and side edges aligned, pin the pocket piece to the cardholder and stitch along sides and across bottom edge.

To Finish

1. Using 3 strands of embroidery floss and a chain stitch (see page 11), create a smiling mouth between the rosy cheeks on the snowman's face.
2. Tack a small curtain ring to the back of each corner for hanging.

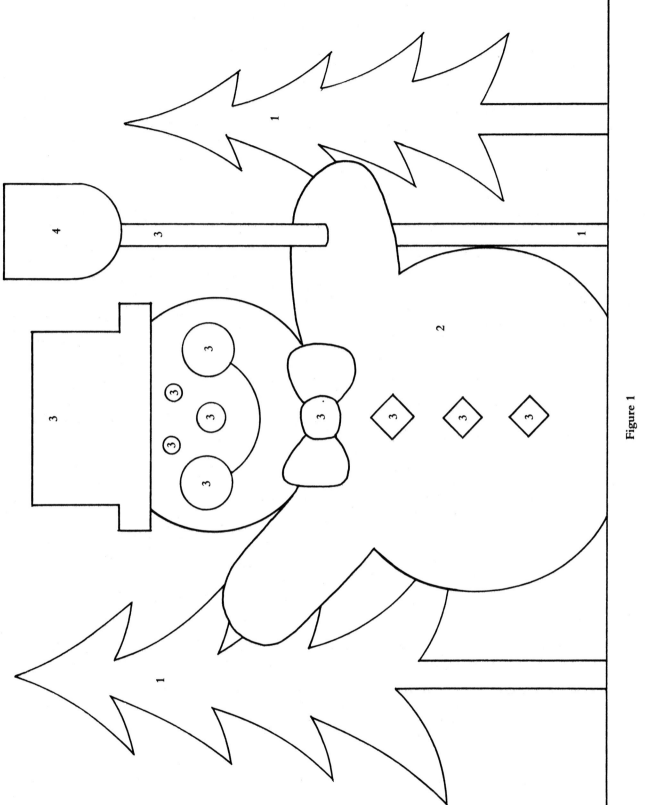

Figure 1

Numbers indicate order in which to attach pieces

109

Jolly Santa Decorations

The Santa motif is a holiday favorite with everyone—young and old. And so we created a charming trio of felt Santa decorations for table, tree, and door.

Jolly Santa

Our Jolly Santa is perfect as a decoration in the center of a bunch of greens or a wreath on the door. He adds just the right sparkle surrounded by red balls. He can also be used as the focal point of Jolly Santa Placemats, page 114. The finished size is 7½ × 8½ inches. A smaller version (shown on page 114) can be made for tree ornaments.

MATERIALS

Small piece of fusible felt in each of the following colors: white, pink, flesh, and black (or use fusible webbing with plain felt)

7½ × 8½-inch piece of plain red felt

Fusible webbing (available in fabric stores) if plain felt is used

Stuffing

8 inches embroidery floss, yarn, or ribbon for hanging

Tracing paper

DIRECTIONS

1. Trace each pattern piece and pin to the color felt indicated on each.
2. If using plain felt, pin the pattern to felt and same-size piece of fusible webbing.
3. Cut out all pieces.

To Assemble

1. Refer to Figure 1. Arrange the eyebrows, eyes, and cheeks on the flesh-colored face.
2. Place a clean cloth over the felt pieces and press with a medium hot iron for 5 seconds.
3. Next, arrange the hair, beard, mouth, and mustache and press in position as before.
4. Arrange the hat and pompon in place and press to fuse.

To Finish

1. Trace the outline of the completed Santa pattern and pin to the piece of plain red felt. Cut out.

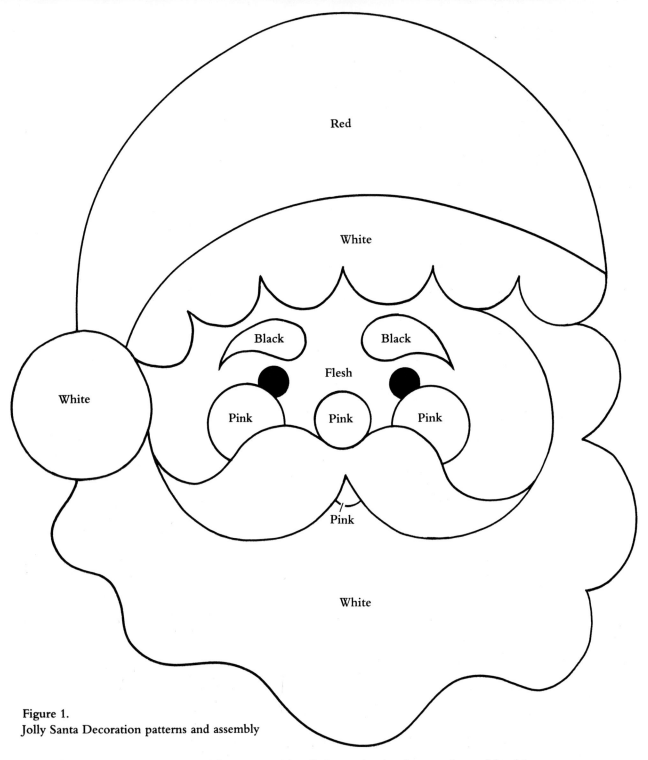

Red

White

Black   Black

Flesh

White

Pink   Pink   Pink

Pink

White

Figure 1.
Jolly Santa Decoration patterns and assembly

2. With wrong sides facing, pin the face to the red backing.
3. Leaving one side of the red hat open for stuffing, stitch around as close to the outside edge as possible.
4. Stuff until puffy. Use the eraser end of a pencil or a crochet hook to push stuffing into all the curves of the beard and point of the hat.
5. Slip-stitch opening closed. Add a loop of embroidery floss, yarn, or ribbon to the top for hanging or attach to greens by pinning from the back.

Jolly Santa Ornaments

These Santa ornaments match the Jolly Santa on page 111, but they are slightly smaller (3½ × 4½ inches) for use on the Christmas tree. They are easy to make because they are identical and you can cut all the pattern pieces at once. The Santa theme is delightful, and small children will love it. Let them help make the ornaments by tracing each of the pattern pieces. After you've cut and ironed all the elements together, a small child should be able to stuff each one before you do the final stitching.

MATERIALS

Small piece of fusible felt in each of the following colors: red, white, pink, flesh, and black (or use fusible webbing with plain felt)

4½ × 5½-inch piece of plain red felt for each ornament

Fusible webbing (available in fabric stores) if plain felt is used
Red embroidery floss for hanging
Stuffing
Tracing paper

DIRECTIONS

Refer to Jolly Santa, page 110. Pattern for Jolly Santa Ornament is on page 115.

To Make in Quantity

If you'd like to fill your tree with these Jolly Santa ornaments it's best to make a template of each pattern piece. Refer to page 8 for transferring the patterns to heavy paper in order to make templates. It is most efficient to do each step for all ornaments at once, rather than to complete one ornament before making another.

1. Determine how many ornaments you will make and how much flesh and red felt you will need for the front and back of each 4½ × 5½-inch piece.

2. Place full-size template on the felt and draw around the outline. Continue to do this over the entire piece of felt. Cut out all pieces.

3. Use each template to draw and cut out as many pieces of each color as needed (see page 112 for colors of pieces).

4. Position each felt piece on the background and continue as for Jolly Santa Decoration, page 110.

Pattern for Jolly Santa Ornaments

Jolly Santa Placemats

A set of four Jolly Santa placemats makes a wonderful gift for the holidays. Everyone loves to set a special table at this special time of year. Or make one placemat for a child to use during the holidays. The octagonal shape adds interest and the blue-and-white polka dot background is intended to look like a snowfall.

All the appliqué pieces are cut from washable fabric. No sewing is required for the appliqué if you use a fusible webbing to attach the fabric pieces. They will not come off in the wash. If they loosen after many washings, simply reapply with more fusible webbing. The finished placemat is 13 × 17 inches.

MATERIALS (for 4 placemats)

1 yard blue polka dot fabric
1 yard red fabric (includes
 backing)
¼ yard white opaque fabric
Scrap pieces of pale pink, deep
 pink, and black fabric

Fusible webbing (available in
 fabric stores)
6½ yards double-fold red bias tape
1 yard thin quilt batting
Tracing paper

DIRECTIONS

1. You'll need a piece of tracing paper slightly larger than 13 × 17 inches. If necessary, tape pieces of paper together to create the size needed. Trace the pattern piece from Figure 2, which is one-quarter of the placemat. Turn the tracing and continue to trace the pattern 3 more times to complete the pattern.
2. You will be cutting 4 pattern pieces from the polka dot fabric and 4 from the red for the backing of each placemat. Plan the layout and pin the pattern to the fabric. Cut out each piece.
3. Trace each appliqué pattern piece (use Jolly Santa pattern, page 112) and pin to the indicated color fabric together with the same size piece of fusible webbing.
4. Cut out 4 of each pattern piece.

To Assemble

1. Center one Santa face on the polka dot background. Place a clean cloth over the face and press with a medium hot iron for 3 seconds to fuse.
2. Arrange the eyebrows, eyes, and cheeks on the face and iron in place as before.
3. Continue with the hair, beard, mouth, and mustache.
4. Finish with the hat, pompon, and nose.
5. Repeat steps 1 through 4 for the remaining 3 placemats.

To Finish

1. Cut 4 pieces of quilt batting, each 13 × 17 inches.
2. With batting between and wrong sides facing, pin the backing and top of the placemat together.
3. Trim the batting to the shape of the placemat.
4. Pin the bias tape all around the outside edge encasing all 3 layers of material. Take a tiny fold in the tape at each corner of the placemat.
5. Stitch around.

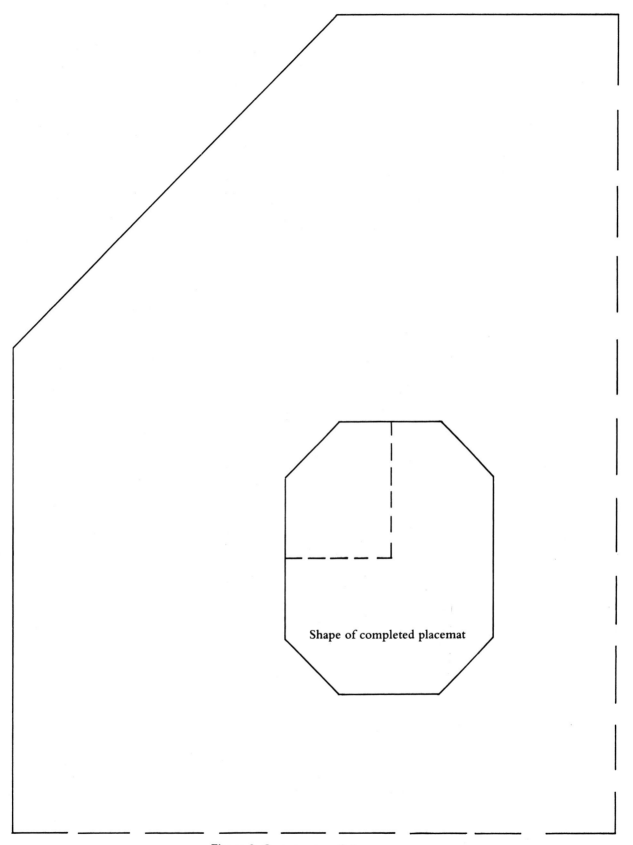

Shape of completed placemat

Figure 2. One-quarter of placemat pattern

Country Geese Tree Skirt

A tree skirt always dresses up the Christmas tree. It's quick and easy to make this skirt sporting appliquéd geese because there's no sewing involved. Also, there's no piecing, as the skirt is made from the width of one piece of felt. The finished size is 44 inches in diameter. If you'd like to make a larger skirt, double the amount of green felt and stitch two pieces together before cutting the circle to size.

MATERIALS (all fabric is 45 inches wide)

1¼ yards plain green felt
½ yard each of white and red fusible felt (or use fusible webbing with plain felt)
Small piece of bright yellow fusible felt

Fusible webbing (available in fabric stores) if plain felt is used
Black embroidery floss
Tracing paper
Heavy paper, such as manila folder

DIRECTIONS

1. Begin by cutting a 44-inch-diameter circle from the green felt. To do this, cut a 46-inch length of string and tape one end to the center of the fabric. Wrap the other end around a pencil and tape securely so you have a length of string 44 inches long. Holding the taped end of the string to the center of the cloth, pull the pencil until the string is taut and draw a circle all around. Cut it out.

2. Trace all pattern pieces on page 120 and transfer to heavy paper to make templates (see page 8).

3. Place the goose template on the white felt and trace around the outline. Make 8.

4. Outline the beak template on the bright yellow felt 8 times. Repeat with each foot template.

5. Cut out all pieces. If using plain felt, pin each pattern piece to felt and fusible webbing and cut together.

To Make Scarves

1. From the red felt cut a piece 12 × 24 inches.

2. Cut 6 white felt strips, each 1 × 24 inches. (If using plain felt, cut each strip together with a piece of fusible webbing).

3. Beginning 1 inch down from the long edge of the red felt, place a white strip across the felt. Place a clean cloth over the felt and fuse with a medium hot iron for 5 seconds.

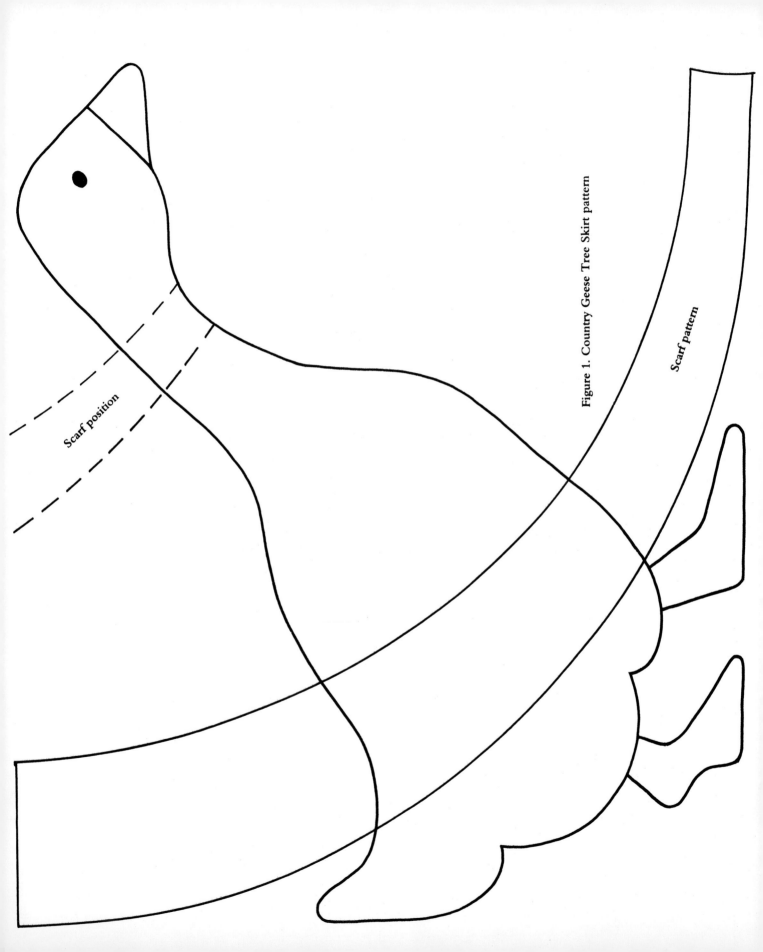

Scarf position

Scarf pattern

Figure 1. Country Geese Tree Skirt pattern

4. Continue to attach white strips every other inch to create a red-and-white striped material.

5. Place the scarf template on the back of the striped felt and trace around the outside edges. Repeat 7 more times.

6. Cut out all striped scarves.

To Assemble

1. Arrange each of the geese so they are evenly spaced around the green felt circle approximately 1½ inches from the bottom edge.

2. Place a clean cloth over each one and press with medium hot iron for 5 seconds to fuse in place.

3. Next, arrange the scarves, beaks, and feet (as shown in Figure 1) and fuse as before.

4. Mark the center of the tree skirt and cut a slit up the back to this point.

5. Cut a circle approximately 3 inches in diameter (or to fit your tree trunk) in the center of the skirt. Arrange around your Christmas tree.

All Aglow

Did you know that some colorful markers work on glass? This opens up a whole slew of opportunities for creating quick-and-easy temporary projects. Acrylic paint washes off glass and china as well, but using markers is as easy as coloring and doesn't require a brush.

Decorate ordinary items like bowls or glasses for the holidays, or windowpanes, then wash away the decorations after the party's over. These decorative hurricane lamps are a cinch to create with Uni POSCA opaque water-soluble markers from Faber Castell. They're available in art stores. If you buy another brand, be sure they are water soluble so you can remove the designs later if desired. When the candles are lit the designs glow from the light behind them. It's a pretty and very easy way to create a centerpiece for your holiday dinner.

MATERIALS

Glass hurricane lamps (available in home centers)
Red, green, and black water-soluble markers

Tracing paper
Tape (optional)

DIRECTIONS

1. Trace the complete design on page 124. Make a slit at the top and bottom of the tracing paper and tape in position inside the hurricane lamp. The slit of the paper will enable it to conform to the shape of the lamp.
2. Place one hand inside the lamp against the tracing paper and use the other hand to fill in the color of each design element. The markers will work well on the glass and can be removed easily with a damp cloth if you make an error.
3. Using the red marker, follow the tracing of the bow and fill in the color on the glass.
4. With green, fill in each holly leaf. With black marker, draw a line down the center of each leaf as indicated on the tracing.

Decorating a Windowpane

1. Cut out each design element as a separate piece.
2. Tape the designs in position on the windowpane and outline each with the appropriate color.
3. Remove the tracing pattern and fill in each color. Where the markers don't cover completely, let dry and go over the area once more.

Pattern for All Aglow glass painting

Clothespin Wreath

A few years ago we designed a clothespin wreath for a Christmas issue of *Ladies Home Journal* magazine. It was such a popular project that we redesigned it slightly and are including the updated version.

Wreaths made from all kinds of material are seen on front doors during the season. Most are made from natural materials, so this clothespin wreath is quite different. Made from two types of clothespins, it is varnished to give it a protective coating for withstanding unpredictable weather conditions. While the ordinary materials used in this project remain recognizable, the wreath is appreciated for its cleverness.

MATERIALS

12 × 12-inch piece of stiff corregated cardboard or Fome-Cor (available in art stores)
1 package one-piece wooden clothespins
1 package spring-type wooden clothespins
White craft glue
10 or 12 silver bells or small Christmas balls
Spray varnish
1½-inch-wide ribbon 24″ long
Small piece of florist's wire
Sprig of greens (optional)
Picture hanging tab

DIRECTIONS

1. Begin by cutting a 10-inch-diameter circle from the cardboard.
2. Next, cut a 5-inch-diameter hole in the center of this circle. You now have a 2½-inch-wide disk that will become the base on which to create the wreath.
3. On the outside edge, slip a one-piece clothespin onto the disk.
4. Next, clip a spring-type clothespin onto the cardboard from the outside edge. Be sure the clothespins are pressed against one another. Note that the spring-type clothespins are not as long as the one-piece clothespins, but the gap will be filled later.
5. Continue to fill the disk by alternating the orientation and kind of clothespin in this way.
6. Next you will add a ring of only one-piece clothespins. Glue them with heads toward the inside edge of the disk between the spring-type clothespins

of the first ring. Each clothespin of the top layer will lie head to toe with the one-piece clothespins of the bottom layer. In this way the heads of the clothespins will surround the inner hole of the wreath.

To Finish

1. Spray the entire wreath with clear varnish. Let dry and recoat if added protection is desired.
2. Glue silver bells or balls so they are evenly spaced between the clothespins around the wreath.
3. Tie a fat bow and secure around a sprig or two of greens if desired. Wire to the center of the bottom of the wreath and hang.
4. Attach the picture hanging tab to the back and secure with strong tape so it can hold the weight of the clothespins when hung.

Shell Wreath

If you've collected shells during a vacation at the beach, here's the perfect way to use them. A shell wreath is simple and elegant. Here on Nantucket Island, shell wreaths are commonplace, most incorporating scallop shells, which represent the winter industry. Any kinds of shells can be used for this project. They can all be the same for a uniform look, as we've done, or different sizes and types. Add a few red beads or Christmas balls and a taffeta bow and nothing could be prettier.

MATERIALS

12 × 12-inch piece of stiff corregated cardboard or Fome-Cor (available in art stores)
Large assortment of shells
Approximately 2 dozen red beads or small Christmas balls
White craft glue or hot-glue gun (available in craft stores, five-and-tens)

12-inch length of 1½-inch-wide taffeta ribbon
Picture hanging tab
Tape

DIRECTIONS

1. Begin by cutting a 10-inch-diameter circle from the cardboard.
2. Next, cut a 5-inch-diameter hole in the center of this circle. You will have a 2½-inch-wide disk which will become the base on which to create the wreath.
3. Beginning at the center of the cardboard, apply a ring of glue around the hole. Arrange the first group of shells around the cardboard so they extend slightly beyond the edge of the cardboard.
4. Continue to glue a ring of shells around the cardboard so that each successive ring of shells overlaps the preceding circle of shells. The last ring of shells should extend slightly beyond the outer rim of the cardboard base.

To Finish

1. When the entire cardboard has been covered with shells, glue the red beads here and there on and between the shells as they look good to you.
2. Let everything dry thoroughly, for about an hour, before lifting the finished wreath.
3. Using the taffeta ribbon, create a generous bow and glue or wire to the bottom portion of the wreath.
4. Attach the picture hanging tab to the back and secure with strong tape so it can hold the weight of the shells when hung.

And All the Trimmings

Wrapping gifts, making greeting cards, and creating ornaments for the Christmas tree are part of what makes the month of December so much fun. Some of us do Christmas crafting all year long, and if you're like me, you start making your gifts in the summertime. But the days between Thanksgiving and Christmas are special. There's excitement in the air like no other time of year.

One of the things I like best about making the trimmings is that they're usually quick-and-easy projects. Most of the materials are simple and readily available and sometimes I can use scraps from other projects. Tree ornaments make great small gifts and bazaar items. It's especially satisfying to fill a tree with handmade ornaments that you add to each year.

Sensational Wraps

It's so easy to design your own wrapping paper and make all your packages special. In fact, it's nicer and less expensive to make your own than to use store-bought. Using simple stencils and colored markers you can decorate plain shiny paper with different Christmas symbols as well as initials, sayings, and names. All the materials for cutting our stencil designs are available in art stores. An alternative to cutting stencil designs is to use Christmas cookie cutters for your patterns. And here's a clever idea I discovered by accident. Last year all the bows on the presents I sent to relatives who live far away got crushed in the mail. This year I'm drawing my bows right on the packages with markers. No ribbons, no crushed bows!

MATERIALS

Colorful markers (a white marker can be used on colored papers)
Stencil paper
X-Acto craft knife
2-inch-high stencil letters (available in craft, art, or five-and-dime stores)

Solid color wrapping paper (or use plain shelf-lining paper, available in rolls)
Ribbons and bells (optional)
Tracing paper
Masking tape

DIRECTIONS

1. If you are using precut stencils or cookie cutters, you're ready to go. If you are using the designs provided, begin by tracing those on pages 132–133.
2. Tape the tracing to the stencil paper and place on a cutting surface.
3. Using the craft knife, follow each traced line and cut through the tracing paper and stencil paper beneath. Remove all cutout pieces.
4. Wrap all your packages with the plain paper.

To Stencil

1. Place a stencil design where you want it on the package and fill in with the desired color marker.
2. For small designs, place the stencil on one side of the package and, using a pencil, draw the design inside all cutout lines of the stencil. Then fill in

with marker color of your choice. Remember to try the white marker on red, green, or blue papers. White is good for creating snowmen or snowflake designs (as blue package in the photograph).

3. To add a message to a package with letters such as "NOEL," trace the letters in position on paper to use as a guide for placing the stencil letters exactly where you want them on the package. Stencil the name of each person on his or her present.

To Finish

Add ribbons, bows, bells, artificial greens, candy canes, etc., to each package. They'll look too good to open.

Pretty Patchwork Cards

One day, while browsing through a boutique, I came across some exquisite greeting cards. The front of each one was decorated with pieced fabric to create an Amish quilt square. This gave me an idea for making my own cards using cut paper to create traditional quilt patterns. It's much easier than cutting and piecing fabric. If you use bright red and green paper you can make your own, very distinctive Christmas cards. I think I might make cards to use all year long. Each card is 5 × 5 inches.

MATERIALS (for 4 cards)

4 sheets of white card paper or Bristol board, each 5 × 10 inches (available in art stores)
1 sheet each of red and green shiny paper

Tracing paper
Rubber cement

DIRECTIONS

Card 1

1. From red paper cut the following: 4 rectangles, each 1 × 2 inches and 1 square 1½ × 1½ inches.
2. Trace the entire design from Card 1.
3. Fold one piece of card paper in half lengthwise. Open the card and lay it flat on your work surface.
4. Place the tracing of the design over the right half of the card (this will be the front). There will be ½ inch of card all around the design. Use your tracing as a placement guide for the paper patchwork pieces.
5. Coat the back of the red pieces with rubber cement and set aside to dry.
6. Using the tracing as a guide, carefully place each pattern piece. When using rubber cement you can't lift and reapply; if you make a mistake you'll need rubber cement remover. When all the pieces have been applied, the extra rubber cement around the design can be removed easily by rubbing over it with a gum eraser (available in art supply stores) or your fingers. The excess cement will pick right up.
7. Refold the card with the design on the front.

Card 2

1. From the red paper cut the following: 4 squares, each 1½ × 1½ inches. Cut each square in half along the diagonal to make 8 triangles.
2. Trace the entire design for Card 2.
3. Follow steps 3 through 7 for Card 1.

Card 3

1. From green paper cut the following: 4 squares, each 1 × 1 inch. Cut each square in half along the diagonal to make 8 triangles.
2. From green paper cut 1 square 2 × 2 inches.
3. Trace the entire design for Card 3.
4. Follow steps 3 through 7 from Card 1.

Card 4

1. Trace the pattern shape for Card 4 and transfer to green paper (see page 8). Cut 4.
2. Trace the entire design for Card 4.
3. Follow steps 3 through 7 for Card 1.

Card 1

Card 2

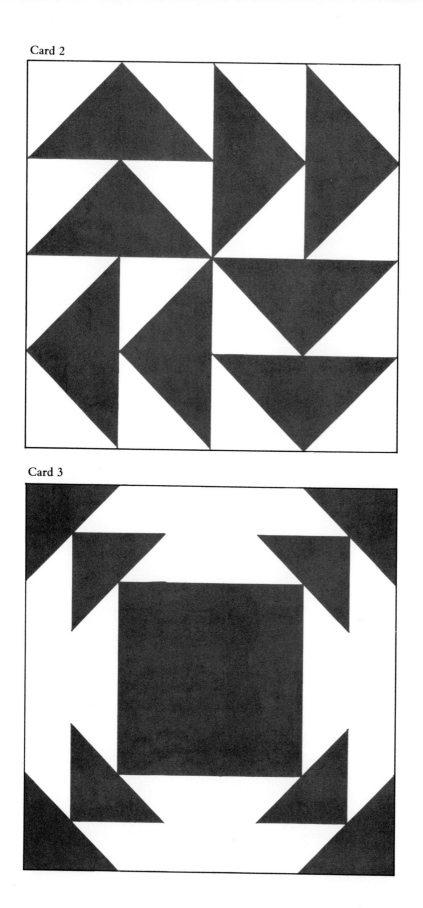

Card 3

Card 4

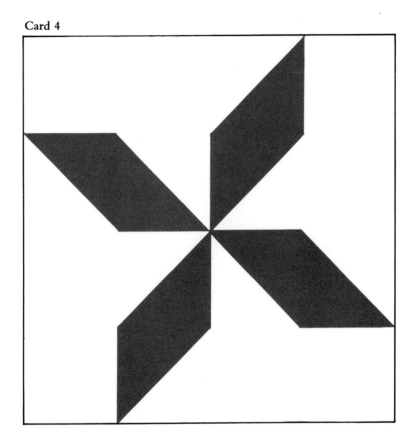

138

Cross-Stitch Cuties

Counted cross-stitch ornaments make wonderful gifts or trimmings for your own tree. Because the designs are small, the projects work up quickly. The dancing Santa was stitched by Liz Putur and the others were made by Suzi Peterson. All were done on 14-count even-weave Aida cloth and are trimmed with lace or colorful piping. All cross-stitch materials are available in craft stores, five-and-tens, and some yarn shops. Always work with a piece of even-weave cloth that is twice the size of the finished ornament so you'll have plenty of fabric around the design while doing your embroidery. This will be more comfortable and make it easy to center the design.

MATERIALS

For all ornaments

Embroidery needle
Backing fabric (can be Aida cloth, felt, or colorful fabric)

Stuffing
Masking tape

Tree ornament (finished size 2 × 3 inches)

14-count red Aida cloth
1 skein embroidery floss of each color: white, green, and yellow

10½ inches lace trim
6 inches ⅛-inch-wide white satin ribbon

Reindeer ornament (finished size 2½ inches in diameter)

14-count white Aida cloth
1 skein embroidery floss of each color: red, brown, and black

8 inches lace trim
8 inches ⅛-inch-wide red satin ribbon

Church ornament (finished size 2½ × 3½ inches)

14-count white Aida cloth
1 skein embroidery floss of each color: gray, red, green, and blue

12½ inches lace trim
8 inches ⅛-inch-wide red satin ribbon

Santa ornament (finished size 3¼ × 5¼ inches)

14-count white Aida cloth
1 skein embroidery floss of each
   color: red, black, navy blue,
   flesh, and green

1 package green or red piping
6 inches ¼-inch-wide red satin
   ribbon

DIRECTIONS

The charts provided for each ornament indicate where to place the stitches in each color to create a design on the even-weave fabric. Each square on the chart represents a square on the cloth.

1. Begin by taping the edges of the cloth so they won't fray.
2. Using a pencil on the even-weave fabric, center and draw a rectangle or circle to the size given for the finished ornament you are making.
3. Refer to the chart for the placement of each color in each square of the fabric.
4. Cut a piece of embroidery floss approximately 18 inches long. Separate the 6 strands and rejoin 3. Thread through the embroidery needle.
5. To find the placement of the first stitch, count up from the bottom of the chart to the first stitch. Count in from the right side edge. Do the same on your fabric, starting from your drawn pencil lines to find the square on the fabric. The chart will indicate the color of this stitch.

To Cross-Stitch

1. Do not make a knot in the end of your floss as you would for regular sewing. Locate the first square and insert your needle into one fabric hole from the underside. Pull it through until you have a 1-inch tail remaining on the underside.
2. Reinsert the needle through the hole diagonally to the right, across the first square on the front of the fabric. Continue to do this, working diagonally across the row, using the same color as indicated on the chart.
3. When you have completed a section of left-to-right slanted stitches, cross back to make each stitch into an X (see page 11). Each time you run out of floss, weave the last bit under a few stitches on the underside to secure the work.

Note: If you are working on an area that has few stitches in each row, you might prefer to cross each stitch as you work it. With this method you have to make sure each stitch is crossed in the same direction so the finished work looks neat. Each hole is worked twice when the stitches are together with no spaces between. When working on isolated stitches, always complete each stitch, end the thread, and move to the next area.

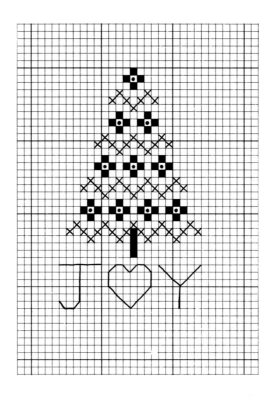

⊠ White

■ Green

☐ Yellow

— Backstitch in white for letters

⊠ Brown

— Backstitch for letters

Black: French knot for eyes, backstitch for antlers

Red: French knot for nose, backstitch for letters

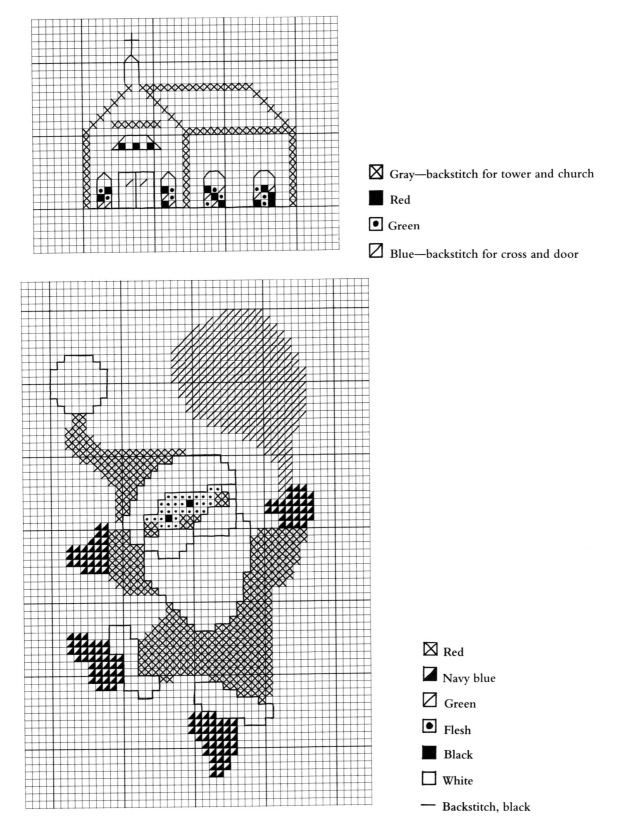

⊠ Gray—backstitch for tower and church

■ Red

⊡ Green

⊘ Blue—backstitch for cross and door

⊠ Red

◪ Navy blue

⊘ Green

⊡ Flesh

■ Black

□ White

— Backstitch, black

Backstitch

Used for outlining, the backstitch (see page 11) looks very much like machine stitching. Stitches are even and close together and often used for stitching sayings, such as "Joy" and "Seasons Greetings." Using 2 strands of floss, bring the needle up from the underside of the fabric and reinsert it a half stitch behind where the thread came through. Bring it back up a half stitch in front of this point. Continue in this way as indicated on the chart for the cross-stitch projects.

French Knot

French knots (see page 11) are used for the reindeer's eyes and nose. Bring the needle out on the right side of the fabric where the stitch is indicated on the chart. Wrap the thread two or three times around the point of the needle and insert the needle close to the spot where the thread came through. Hold the knot in place and pull the thread to the wrong side.

To Finish All Ornaments

1. When all designs have been completed, remove the tape from around the edges.
2. Cut out each ornament ¼ inch larger than the drawn lines all around. This is your seam allowance.
3. Cut a piece of fabric for backing same size.
4. With raw edges aligned, pin the lace trim or piping around the front of the ornament. Stitch around.
5. With right sides facing and raw edges aligned, pin the front and back pieces together with the trim between, leaving the top edge open.
5. Stitch around 3 sides and 4 corners of the fabric.
6. Clip the corners and turn right side out. Steam-press from wrong side.
7. Fill with stuffing. Fold the ribbon in half and insert the raw ends into the center of the top opening. Slip-stitch the opening closed.

Colorful Felt Decorations

All the designs for these projects were cut from iron-on felt, but you can use regular felt combined with fusible webbing for no-sew, quick-and-easy projects. The same shapes are used as stocking decorations, tree ornaments, and package gift tags. This creates a matching theme.

MATERIALS

½ yard white felt
Piece of fusible red felt 4 × 6 inches (or use fusible webbing with plain felt)
Small pieces of fusible felt in the following colors: red, green, blue, and gold
Fusible webbing if plain felt is used

1 package green or red piping
1 skein black embroidery floss
White card paper for gift tags
Tracing paper
Heavy paper, such as manila folder

Stocking

DIRECTIONS

1. Trace the stocking pattern (including cuff), which is shown full size in Figure 1. Pin to the white felt and cut 2.
2. Trace the cuff section of the stocking and pin to the 4 × 6 inch piece of red felt. Cut out. If using plain felt, cut a matching piece of fusible webbing.
3. Pin the cuff in position on the front of one stocking piece (with fusible webbing, if used, between) and press with a medium hot iron for 5 seconds.
4. Trace all appliqué pattern pieces. Pin each to the corresponding color felt and cut out.
5. Refer to Figure 1 and arrange the appliqués on the front of the stocking piece with the cuff as shown.
6. Place a clean cloth over each element and press with the iron as before.
7. Using 3 strands of embroidery floss and a running stitch (see page 11), embroider the details on the drum and the eyes and mouth on the star.

To Finish

1. Cut a piece of piping, ribbon, or decorative trim slightly longer than the width of the bottom edge of the cuff. Pin across with edges tucked under at each end. Stitch across.
2. With wrong sides facing and piping between, pin the front and back of the stocking together, leaving the top edge open.
3. Cut a 4-inch length of piping and fold in half to make a loop. Insert the raw ends between the stocking pieces at the back top edge.
4. Start at this point and stitch around the stocking as close to the outer edge as possible, leaving the top edge open.

Ornaments

DIRECTIONS

1. Trace all patterns on page 150 and transfer the designs to heavy paper to make templates (see page 8). If making one ornament, pin the tracing to the corresponding colors of felt. Cut 2 for each ornament (1 for the back and 1 for the front). If using templates, place each one on the felt and draw around the outline twice for each ornament.
2. Use the embroidery floss to stitch the details on the drum and the star as you did for the stocking.
3. Cut a 4-inch length of embroidery floss and with the raw ends between the felt at one corner of the ornament, fuse the back and front ornament pieces together with a medium hot iron for 5 seconds.

Gift Tags

DIRECTIONS

1. Trace and cut one piece of felt for each gift tag. If you're making several of one design, see directions for making templates page 8 and refer to step 1 for making ornaments.
2. Add embroidery details to the drum and stars as for ornaments.
3. Measure and cut a 3-inch square for each gift tag needed.
4. Center a felt appliqué piece on each card, place a clean cloth over the felt, and press with a hot iron for 3 seconds. (The fusible felt or fusible webbing will adhere to paper in only 3 seconds).
5. Punch a hole in one corner of the card, thread with embroidery floss or ribbon, and tie to package.

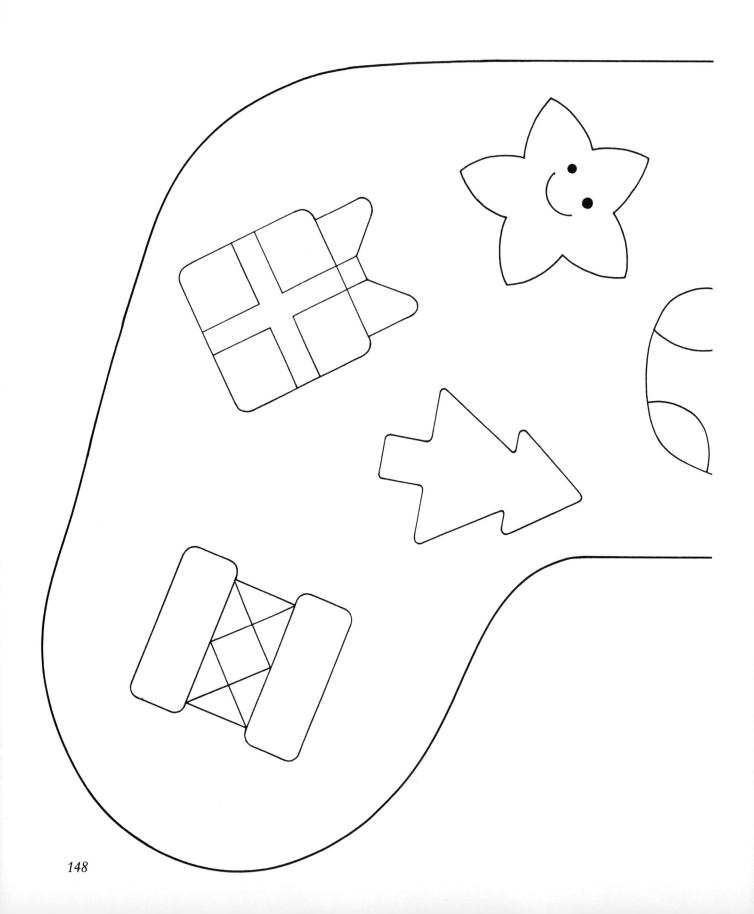

Figure 1. Trace stocking patterns and tape sections
together to make complete pattern. Trace appliqué patterns

Patterns for ornaments and gift tags

Happy Hearts

Woven hearts decorate many Christmas trees in Scandinavia. This is a traditional ornament that decorates Else Knudsen's tree in her hometown in Norway. While living on Nantucket last year she did some crafting for us in the studio (see her knit hat and scarf on page 31) and made these ornaments to show how quick and easy they are. We used red, white, green, and blue felt, but you can make them with any color combination. The pattern given is for the smaller version, which is 3½ × 4 inches. This is a nice size for a tree ornament.

MATERIALS

2 different colored pieces of felt,
 each 3 × 8 inches

Stuffing
Tracing paper

DIRECTIONS

1. Trace the pattern from Figure 1.
2. Pin this pattern to each piece of felt and cut one of each color.
3. Pin the pattern to the felt and use it as a guide to cut along the straight lines to create slits in each piece of felt.
4. Fold each felt piece in half as shown in Figure 2.
5. Weave the folded ends of the felt pieces in and out of each other to create a checkerboard weave as shown in Figure 3. This creates the front and back of each ornament.

To Finish

1. Pin the edges of the front and back together.
2. From the leftover felt of one color, cut a strip ½ × 4 inches for the hanging loop.
3. Fold in half lengthwise and insert the ends between the front and back at the top of the heart.
4. Machine- or hand-stitch around the outside edge, leaving a small opening at the top for stuffing.
5. Fill with stuffing and stitch opening closed.

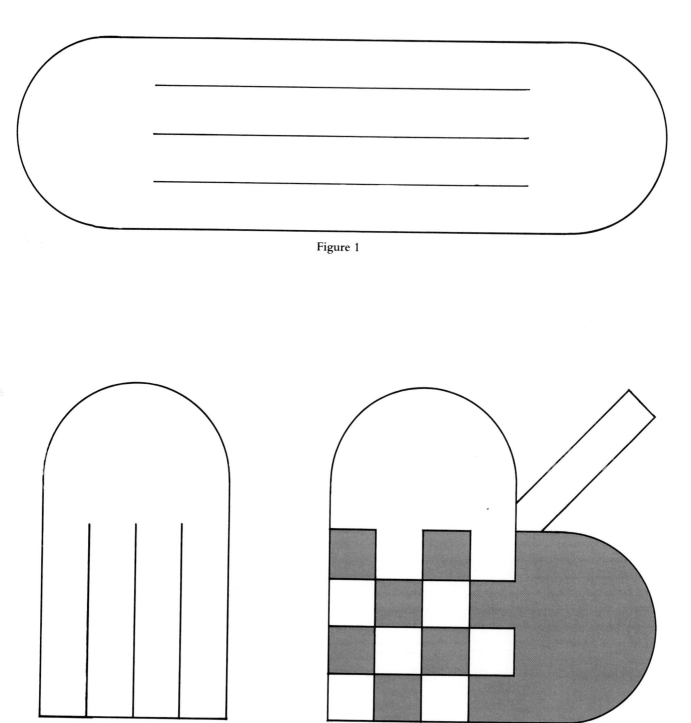

Figure 1

Figure 2

Figure 3

Toyland Soldiers

Felt soldiers stand at attention in their bright red, green, and blue uniforms (see photo on previous page). They are delightful ornaments and easy to make from cut pieces of felt. If you'd like to create a Christmas theme, consider making these ornaments and the NOEL banner on page 93.

MATERIALS

Small pieces of fusible felt in the following colors: red, navy blue, black, yellow, pink, green, white, and brown (or use glue with plain felt)

2 × 8-inch piece of blue felt for background of each ornament
Black embroidery floss
Gold cord or floss for hanging
Tracing paper

DIRECTIONS

Note: All appliqué pieces are given full size. No seam allowance is needed.

1. Trace the standing soldier from Figure 1 on page 95.
2. Cut full pattern from 2 × 8-inch piece of blue felt.
3. Trace each pattern piece for the soldier.
4. Pin the traced patterns to the color felt indicated on the pattern pieces and cut out.
5. Arrange all the pieces on the blue piece for the full soldier as shown and fuse with a medium hot iron for 5 seconds. Or glue each piece of plain felt in position.
6. Using 3 strands of black embroidery floss make 2 small French knots (see page 11) for the eyes.

Back

1. Cut all pieces for the jacket, hands, and hat as for the front.
2. Cut the face piece from brown for the back of the head. Do not cut pink cheeks or black shoes.
3. The bottom portion of the blue backing becomes the pants. Position and fuse or glue each piece of the jacket on the blue background where indicated.
4. Glue or fuse the brown head piece above the jacket and add the hat pieces.

To Finish

1. Using 3 strands of black embroidery floss and a chain stitch (see page 11) sew a line down the center of the blue pants to create the pants legs.
2. Attach a gold cord or embroidery floss to the top for hanging.

Jolly Penguins

Black-and-white penguins with fat red bow ties make adorable ornaments (see photo on page 157). We designed two versions, one facing forward and one facing the side, to add variety. Each felt penguin is slightly stuffed to give it a rounded, puffy look, which you'd expect on a penguin. The finished size is 3 × 5 inches.

MATERIALS

Small pieces of felt in the following colors: black, white, gold, and red
Stuffing
Small piece each of black and red embroidery floss
White craft glue
Tracing paper
Heavy paper, such as manila folder

DIRECTIONS

Note: No seam allowance is needed for felt.
1. Trace the patterns and transfer each to heavy paper for templates (see page 8).
2. To make the front piece: On white felt, draw around the entire penguin template and cut out.
3. To make the back piece: On black felt, draw around the entire penguin template and cut out.
4. To make the front coat: On black felt, draw around the template and cut out.
5. To make the feet: On gold felt, draw around the templates, add ¼ inch to the straight edge of each where it will be inserted in the body, and cut out.
6. For the bow ties: On red felt, draw around each template and cut out.
7. For the mouth: On gold felt, draw around the template and cut out.
8. For the beak: On gold felt, draw around the template, add ¼ inch to the straight edge where it will be inserted in the body, and cut out.
9. Using black felt, cut small circles for the eyes.

To Assemble

1. Refer to Figure 1 and glue the black coat piece in position over the white body.

2. Next, glue the red bow in position on the front of the penguin as shown in Figure 1. Refer to Figure 2 and glue the bow tie in position on the penguin facing sideways.

3. Add the eyes in the same way.

4. For the front version: Glue the mouth in position and, using 3 strands of embroidery floss, work a chain stitch (see page 11) across the mouth.

5. For both penguins: Pin the front and back pieces together with the feet or foot tucked in position between the layers at the bottom.

6. For the sideways penguin: Tuck the beak between layers just above the bow tie.

7. Use a plain or zigzag stitch around the edge of each penguin, leaving the top of the head open for stuffing.

To Finish

1. Stuff each penguin so he isn't too full, but nicely rounded.

2. Cut a 6-inch piece of red embroidery floss and fold in half to make a loop.

3. Insert the ends inside the top opening and stitch closed.

Figure 1

Figure 2

156

Silky Stars

At Christmastime the five-and-tens and craft stores carry a variety of crafting materials not always found at other times of the year, including bright colored sequins and sparkles, silver and gold papers, and glitter paint in tubes. It's fun to experiment with new products because it offers a range of new creative crafting possibilities. While browsing through a large discount store I came upon a selection of glitter paint and glitter trimmings which sparked the idea for painting happy faces on silky stars made from acetate (see photo on previous page). It's really easy to make a whole bunch, and the kids will love painting the face on each one. The finished size is 7½ inches.

MATERIALS

½ yard red acetate
1 yard gold ribbon or cord
Stuffing
1 tube gold glitter paint

Tracing paper
Heavy paper, such as manila
 folder

DIRECTIONS

1. Trace the pattern, opposite, and transfer to heavy paper for template (see page 8).
2. Place the template on the red acetate and draw around the outline 10 times to make 5 stars.
3. Cut 5 pieces of gold ribbon, each 6 inches long.
4. With right sides facing and raw edges aligned, pin 2 star pieces together.
5. Using a ¼-inch seam allowance, stitch around leaving the side of one point open for turning.
6. Clip into the seam allowance between each point, then turn right side out. Use a blunt pencil or crochet hook to push out each point.
7. Press with a warm iron.

To Make Faces

1. Refer to the pattern for placement of the face, but faces can be drawn freehand by a child and will always look good.
2. Place the star on a flat, hard surface with the open point at the top. Using the tube of glitter paint, squirt a smiling mouth and 2 dots for eyes.
3. Let dry thoroughly.

To Finish

1. Stuff each star so it is puffy.
2. Fold the gold ribbon or cord in half lengthwise to create a loop and insert the ends into the top of the open point.
3. Stitch opening closed.

Dynamo Dinosaurs

These jaunty, colorful dinosaurs turned out to be so much fun that my friends and I had a pre-Christmas party and spent the evening making a whole bunch of them. Whoever came into the studio wanted to make a dinosaur. One woman we know wants to make them for her tree and then use them as a mobile over her baby's crib. We thought this was a great idea and one that will extend the use of the project. It would even make a nice Christmas gift.

MATERIALS

Assortment of bright-colored felt
   pieces
Stuffing
Black embroidery floss

White craft glue
Tracing paper
Heavy paper, such as manila
   folder

DIRECTIONS

1. Trace the patternson pages 162–163 and transfer to heavy paper for templates (see page 8).
2. Outline each dinosaur template on a piece of bright-color felt. Make 2 (1 piece for the back, 1 for the front).
3. Using another color felt, outline the template for the spine (for the dinosaurs that have spines) and add ¼ inch to the curved edge that will be inserted into the body.
4. Cut out all shapes.
5. Refer to Figure 1 and, using 3 strands of black embroidery floss and a chain stitch (see page 11), sew the mouth and eyes where indicated.
6. Cut small circles from bright-colored felt and glue at random onto the front of the dinosaur.

To Finish

1. Pin the front and back of each dinosaur together, with the spine, if used, in between as shown.
2. Stitch around the outside edge, leaving a small opening at the top of each one for stuffing.
3. Fill loosely with stuffing. Use the eraser end of a pencil or a crochet hook to push stuffing into the points and narrow neck areas.
4. Cut a piece of embroidery floss 6 inches long. Fold in half to make a loop and insert the ends into the center of each opening.
5. Stitch opening closed.

Mini Knit Stockings

These little stockings are knit from scraps of yarn. We combined colors to make the heel and toe of each one a different color than the body. These were made by Gita Lundgren and each is 4 inches long. Fill each with a tiny present or candies, then hang on the tree.

MATERIALS

Small amounts of 4-ply knitting worsted yarn in bright colors

Knitting needles: #6 (4 mm)

DIRECTIONS

Using main color (MC), cast on 25 stitches.
Knit 2 inches of ribbing (knit 1, purl 1).
Attach contrasting color (CC). With first 8 sts only, knit 1 inch in stockinette stitch (k 1 row, p 1 row).

Turn Heel

Starting at the outside edge:
K 1 st, k 2 together, k 1, turn, return purling.
K 2 sts, k 2 tog, k 1, turn, return purling.
K 3 sts, k 2 tog, k 1, turn, return purling.
K 3, k 2 tog (4 sts on right-hand needle) and pick up 4 sts on inside edge of heel. Leave the 8 sts on holder, along with next 9 sts.
Follow same procedure for 8 sts on left side, as follows:
Attach MC and work in stockinette st for 1 inch. Starting at outside edge:
P 1, p 2 tog, p 1, turn, return knitting.
P 2, k 2 tog, p 1, turn, return knitting.
P 3, k 2 tog, p 1, turn, return knitting.
P 3, p 2 tog (4 sts on right-hand needle) and pick up 4 sts on inside edge of heel. Pick up all other sts from holder (total 25 sts).
Attach MC and work 2 rows stockinette st.
Next Row: K 7, k 2 tog, k 7, k 2 tog, k 7 (23 sts).
Next Row: Purl.
Next Row: K 6, k 2 tog, k 7, k 2 tog, k 6 (21 sts).
Next Row: Purl.
Work next 2 rows in stockinette st.

Toe

Join CC and work 2 rows in stockinette st.

Next Row: K 1, k 2 tog, k 7, k 2 tog, k 6, k 2 tog, k 1 (18 sts).

Next Row: Purl.

Next Row: K 1, k 2 tog, k 5, k 2 tog, k 5, k 2 tog, k 1 (15 sts).

Next Row: Purl.

Next Row: K 1, k 2 tog, k 2, k 2 tog, k 1, k 2 tog, k 2, k 2 tog, k 1 (11 sts).

Pull yarn through remaining 11 sts. Sew seam.

Crochet Critters

Using a teddy bear theme you can make ornaments and matching stockings that will delight children. The body of the stocking is made by joining granny squares and the toe is made in the shape of a teddy bear's head. Make Mr. and Mrs. Santa Claus finger puppets in their gingerbread house as a tree decoration. On Christmas day the ornaments become children's gifts. These delightful crocheted cuties were designed for us by Anne Lane.

Teddy Bear Ornament

The twin teddies are perfect ornaments for a whimsical theme. Each child will claim one for his or her own so you might like to make each collar a different color. These teddy bear heads are made with light brown yarn, but if you have leftover dark brown yarn it will look just as good. Add a tiny bell around each teddy's neck. Or a bow tie. The eyes are made with beads, but if you're making this for young children, consider embroidering the face.

MATERIALS

Knitting worsted-weight yarn: ½ oz. each of red, white, and light brown
2-inch-diameter Styrofoam ball
Small amount of stuffing
12 inches gold cord
6 inches ⅛-inch-wide white satin ribbon for around neck
Black 6-strand embroidery floss
Yarn needle
2 black beads for eyes
Small bell
Crochet hook: F/5 (4 mm)

DIRECTIONS

Head

Using brown yarn and starting at the top of the head, chain 2.
Rnd 1: Make 6 single crochet in 2nd ch from hook. *Do not join rounds.* Carry a piece of contrasting color yarn between first and last sc to mark the beginning of the rnds.

Rnd 2: Increase in each sc around (12 sc).

Rnd 3: ★ Sc in first sc, inc in next sc. Repeat from ★ around (18 sc).

Rnd 4: ★ Sc in first 2 sc, inc in next sc. Rep from ★ around (24 sc).

Rnds 5 through 10: Work even on 24 sc.

Rnd 11: ★ Sc in first 2 sc, decrease over next 2 sc. Repeat from ★ around (18 sc).

Rnd 12: Insert the Styrofoam ball. Working around the ball, ★ sc in the first sc, decrease over next 2 sc. Repeat from ★ around (12 sc).

Rnd 13: Dec 6 sc spaced evenly around (6 sc).

Rnd 14: Work even on 6 sc. Fasten off brown yarn and join red yarn.

Rnd 15: Ch 3 (to count as a double crochet) in the first sc, 2 dc. In the next sc and each sc around, make 3 dc. Join last dc to the top of ch 3 with a slipstitch (18 dc).

Rnd 16: Ch 3 (to count as a dc), in the first dc make 1 dc. In the next dc and each dc around, make 2 dc. Join the last dc to the top of ch 3 with a sl st (36 dc). Fasten off red yarn and join white yarn.

Rnd 17: (Work in *back loops only*.) Make 3 sc in each dc around (108 sc). Fasten off, leaving a 12-inch length of yarn for sewing. Fold the "body" in half and stitch firmly through.

Face

Using brown yarn, ch 3.

Row 1: Sc in the 2nd and 3rd ch from the hook. Ch 1 and turn.

Row 2: Work even on 2 sc. Ch 1 and turn.

Row 3: Inc in both sc (4 sc). Ch 1 and turn.

Rows 4 through 6: Work even on 4 sc. Ch 1 and turn at the end of each row.

Row 7: Dec 2 sc over the 4 sc (2 sc). Ch 1 and turn.

Row 8: Work even on 2 sc. Fasten off, leaving a 12-inch length of yarn for sewing the face to the head.

Ears (Make 2)

With brown yarn, ch 2.

Row 1: Make 5 sc in the 2nd ch from the hook. Ch 1 and turn.

Row 2: Sc in the first sc, inc in each of the next 3 sc, sc in last sc (8 sc). Leave a 6-inch length of yarn for sewing the ears to the head and fasten off.

To Finish

1. Stuff the face firmly and sew to the head. Using 3 strands of black embroidery floss and a satin stitch take several stitches at the tip of the nose and use a running stitch or backstitch to make the mouth. (See page 11 for embroidery stitches.)

2. Sew black beads in position for the eyes, or use the satin stitch to embroider eyes.

3. Thread the bell onto the satin ribbon and tie around the bear's neck.

Figure 1. Teddy Bear Ornament assembly

4. Position an ear on each side of the top of the head as shown in Figure 1 and stitch in place.

5. Run the length of gold cord through the top of the head and tie a loop for hanging the ornament on your tree.

Teddy Bear Stocking

Make a darling granny-square bear stocking for your favorite child. There are 13 squares, each 3½ inches. Use bright red and green Christmas colors with white for each center motif. This is an easy take-along project and a guaranteed success at fund-raising bazaars.

MATERIALS

Knitting worsted-weight yarn: 3 ozs. red (A), 1 oz. of each of green (B), white (C), and brown

Small scrap of black felt for the nose

Black embroidery floss for the mouth

Yarn needle

2 small wiggle eyes

Crochet hooks: H/8 (5 mm) and F/5 (4 mm)

DIRECTIONS

Granny-Square Pattern (Make 13)

Working with size H hook and color C, chain 4; join with a slipstitch to form ring.

Rnd 1: Ch 3 (to count as a double crochet), make 2 dc in ring; ch 2. ★ Make 3 dc in ring; ch 2. Repeat from ★ 2 times (12 dc). Join to the top of ch 3 with a sl st. Fasten off C and join B to any ch-2 space.

Rnd 2: Ch 3 (to count as a dc), make 2 dc, ch 2, make 3 dc in same space; ch 1. ★ In the next ch-2 space make 3 dc, ch 2, 3 dc; ch 1. Repeat from ★ 2 times (24 dc). Join to the top of ch 3 with a sl st. Fasten off B and join A to any ch-2 space.

Rnd 3: Ch 3 (to count as a dc), make 2 dc, ch 2, make 3 dc in same space, ch 1, make 3 dc in the ch-1 space of Rnd 2; ch 1. ★ In the next ch-2 space make 3 dc, ch 2, 3 dc; ch 1 and make 3 dc in the next ch-1 space of Rnd 2; ch 1. Repeat from ★ 2 times (36 dc). Join to the top of ch 3 with a sl st. Fasten off A.

Granny-Square Assembly

Refer to the assembly diagram (Figure 2) for arrangement of squares. Using color A take neat overcast stitches through the *back loops only* of Rnd 3 to sew squares together to make rows as follows:

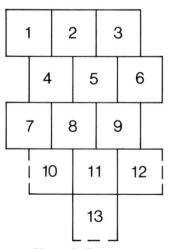

Figure 2. Granny squares assembly diagram

1. Sew Squares 1, 2, and 3 together to make Row 1.

2. Sew Squares 4, 5, and 6 together, then 7, 8, and 9, ending with 10, 11, and 12.

3. Stagger rows as shown in Figure 2 and stitch together.

4. Sew the left side edge of Square 1 to the right side edge of Square 3; the left side edge of Square 4 to the right side edge of Square 6; the left side edge of Square 7 to the right side edge of Square 9. Leave the last row (Squares 10, 11, and 12) open.

5. Stitch any gaps remaining in the horizontal seams between rows.

6. Join the top edge of Square 13 to the bottom edge of Square 11. Then stitch the side edges of Square 13 to the bottom edges of Squares 10 and 12.

Top Border and Hanging Loop

Join white yarn to the top of the stocking.

Rnd 1: Working with size H hook, single crochet around top edge of the stocking. At the end of this rnd, ch 12; join last ch to the first sc of the rnd with a sl st.

Rnd 2: Sc around the top of the stocking and over 12 sc of hanging loop.

Rnd 3: Sc around top of stocking. Fasten off. The granny-square body of the stocking is now complete; you are ready to crochet the toe bear head.

Head

Using brown yarn and size F hook, ch 2.

Rnd 1: Make 6 sc in 2nd ch from the hook. *Do not join rounds.* Carry a piece of contrasting color yarn between the first and last sc to mark the beginning of the rnds.

Rnd 2: Work even on 6 sc.

Rnd 3: Increase in each sc around (12 sc).

Rnd 4: Work even on 12 sc.

Rnds 5 through 8: Inc 6 sc spaced evenly in each rnd (36 sc in Rnd 8).

Rnds 9 through 15: Work even on 36 sc. At end of Rnd 15 end off brown yarn and join red yarn.

Rnds 16 through 18: Work even on 36 sc. Fasten off at end of Rnd 18.

Ears (Make 2)

Using brown yarn and size F hook, ch 2.

Row 1: Make 5 sc in the 2nd ch from the hook. Ch 1 and turn.

Row 2: Sc in the first sc, inc over each of the next 3 sc, sc in the last sc (8 sc). Ch 1 and turn.

Row 3: Sc in the first 2 sc, inc over each of the next 4 sc, sc in the last 2 sc (12 sc). Leaving a 10-inch length of yarn for sewing, fasten off.

Figure 3. Teddy Bear Stocking assembly

Figure 4. Features on face

To Finish

1. Stitch the head to the bottom opening of the stocking (see Figure 3).
2. Stitch or fasten eyes to the head.
3. Cut a small circle of black felt and stitch or glue to the top of the nose.
4. Sew ears to each side of the top of the head as shown in Figure 4.
5. Using 3 strands of black embroidery floss and a running stitch or back-stitch (see page 11) embroider a smiling mouth as shown in Figure 4.

Finger Puppets in a House

Santa and Mrs. Claus are both toy finger puppets and tree ornaments. They fit inside the house, which opens at the top and has a hanging loop. It can be worn on a belt as a purse or hung on the tree. Each puppet is 3½ inches tall and the house measures 4 × 4½ inches to the peak of the roof.

MATERIALS

Knitting worsted-weight yarn:
   ½ oz. white, 1 oz. red, small
    amount of pink
Scraps of green and red felt

Yarn needle
White craft glue
4 wiggle eyes ¼ inch in diameter
Crochet hook: F/5 (4 mm)

DIRECTIONS

House (Make 2)

Using red yarn, chain 16.
Row 1: Single crochet in 2nd ch from the hook and in remaining 14 ch (15 ch). Ch 1 and turn.
Rows 2 through 12: Work even on 15 sc. Ch 1 and turn at end of each row.
Row 13: (Beginning of roof shaping) Decrease over first 2 sc, sc in 11 sc, dec over last 2 sc (13 sc). Ch 1 and turn.
Rows 14 through 18: Dec 1 sc at the beginning and end of each row (3 sc on Row 18). Ch 1 and turn at end of each row.
Row 19: Pull up a loop in each of the remaining 3 sc, yarn over and through all lps on hook. Fasten off.
With white yarn, start at Row 12 and working side-bottom-side-roof, sc around entire house. Leaving a 16-inch length of yarn for sewing, fasten off.

HANDLE

With red yarn, ch 3.

Row 1: Sc in 2nd ch from hook and in last ch (2 sc). Ch 1 and turn.

Rows 2 through 24: Work even on 2 sc. Ch 1 and turn at end of each row *except* at the end of Row 24. Fasten off.

Assembly

1. Using white yarn and an overcast stitch, sew sides and bottom of house pieces together.

2. Refer to Figure 5. To make gingerbread trim on the front of one house piece, use white yarn and blanket-stitch (see page 11) across Row 11 as follows: Insert the yarn needle above and to the right of the starting point and bring it out in line with the last stitch on the line, keeping the yarn behind the point of the needle. Continue working from left to right.

3. Using white yarn, outline the windows and door in chain stitch (see page 11).

4. Cut a circle for the wreath from the green felt.

5. Cut 2 tree-shaped triangles from green felt.

6. Stitch the wreath and the trees in position on the front of the house and add a red yarn bow to the wreath.

7. Stitch the edges of the handle to the inside of each roof peak.

Figure 5. Finger Puppets in a House

Santa and Mrs. Claus

PATTERN (Make 2)
With pink yarn, ch 2.
Rnd 1: Make 6 sc in 2nd ch from hook. *Do not join rounds.* Carry a piece of contrasting color yarn between the first and last sc to mark the beginning of the rnds.
Rnd 2: Inc in each sc around (12 sc).
Rnds 3 through 6: Work even on 12 sc. At end of Rnd 6, fasten off pink yarn and join red yarn.
Rnds 7 through 12: Work even on 12 sc. Fasten off at the end of Rnd 12.

To Finish

SANTA
1. Glue eyes to head.
2. Using scrap of red yarn and a running stitch (see page 11), embroider a smiling mouth.
3. Cut 2 little triangles of red felt for the hat. Stitch the 2 pieces together along the side edges. Stitch onto the top of Santa's head.
4. Using white yarn and yarn needle, make small loops all around the face for Santa's beard.

MRS. CLAUS
1. Glue eyes to head.
2. Using red yarn and running stitch, embroider a smiling mouth.
3. For hair: Cut 20 pieces of white yarn, each 6 inches long. Using a back-stitch (see page 11), sew one end of each strand to the top of the head. Tie each bunch of yarn at the sides of the head with red yarn. Trim where necessary.

Winter Wonderland

Crochet a collection of little ornaments to create a winter wonderland scene on a mantel, on your tree, or as a centerpiece for your holiday dinner. These little ornaments, designed for us by Mary Smith, make delightful gifts or bazaar best sellers. Make them to give each of your guests as a take-home gift at Christmastime.

Tree Bear

Little teddy bears make adorable tree ornaments. They are quick and easy and can be made with scraps of yarn. Use brown, tan, white, or colored yarn and make the scarves all different colors.

MATERIALS

Knitting worsted-weight yarn:
½ oz. brown; small amount of
red and black

Small amount of stuffing
Yarn needle
Crochet hook: F/5 (4 mm)

DIRECTIONS

Head

Chain 4. Join with slipstitch.
Rnd 1: Work 6 single crochet in ring. *Do not join,* but work around in a spiral fashion. Carry a piece of contrasting color yarn between the first and last sc to mark the beginning of the rounds.
Rnd 2: Sc in 1, 2 sc in 1 around.
Rnd 3: 2 sc, 2 sc in 1 around (12 sts).
Rnds 4 and 5: Sc around.
Rnd 6: 7 sc in the next sc, sc, 7 sc in next sc, continue sc around to first ear.
Rnd 7: In back of ear work 3 sc across, 3 sc across back of ear, sc in ear.
Rnd 8: Using the stitches in back of the ear, sc around and decrease 4 st spaced evenly in this rnd.
Stuff the head with filling.
Rnd 9: 1 sc, 1 dec around. Fasten off. Sew back of head closed.

Body

Ch 6, join.
Rnd 1: Sc around.
Rnd 2: 2 sc in 1, 1 sc (9 sts).
Rnd 3: 2 sc in 1, 2 sc (12 sts).
Rnd 4: Repeat Rnd 2 (18 sts).
Rnds 5 through 10: Sc around, sc bottom edge together (9 sts).

Legs

At the bottom edge of the body, ★ work 4 sc across. Ch 1 and turn. Rep from ★ 4 times. Work 6 sc in 2nd st. Sl st to last sc. Fasten off. Rep for other leg.

Arms

Ch 4, join.
Rnd 1: Work 6 sc in ring. Continue working sc around for Rnds 2 through 5. Fasten off.

To Finish

1. Stuff body.
2. Sew arms and head to body.
3. Using black yarn and satin stitch (see page 11), embroider eyes and nose.

Scarf

With red yarn, ch 15 or desired length for scarf. Tie around bear's neck.

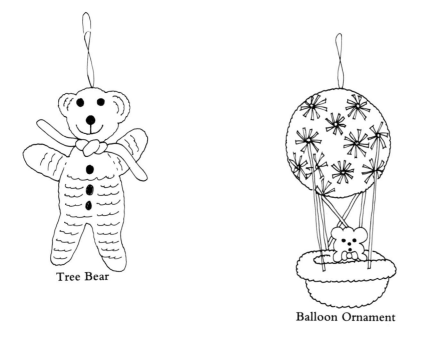

Tree Bear

Balloon Ornament

Balloon Ornament

Everyone loves teddy bears. This balloon ornament holds a basket filled with two miniature teddies that will look darling on your tree. The teddy bears are available in novelty stores. The balloon is decorated with five-and-dime-store sequins. This ornament is especially good for holding small gifts on the tree.

MATERIALS

Knitting worsted-weight yarn: ½ oz. each of colors A (balloon) and B (basket)
2½-inch-diameter Styrofoam ball
24 inches ⅛-inch-wide ribbon
12 inches gold cord

2 small figures
Sequins or other trim
Pins
Crochet hooks: F/5 (4 mm) and steel hook 00 (4 mm)

DIRECTIONS

Balloon

Beginning with size F hook and color A, start at the top of the balloon and chain 2.

Rnd 1: Make 6 sc in the 2nd ch from the hook. *Do not join rounds.* Carry a piece of contrasting color yarn between the first and last sc to mark the beginning of the rounds.

Rnd 2: Increase in each sc around (12 sc).

Rnd 3: ★ Sc in first sc, inc in next sc. Repeat from ★ around (18 sc).

Rnd 4: ★ Sc in first 2 sc, inc in next sc. Rep from ★ around (24 sc).

Rnds 5 through 12: Work even on 24 sc.

Rnd 13: ★ Sc in first 2 sc, decrease over next 2 sc. Rep from ★ around (18 sc).

Rnd 14: Insert Styrofoam ball. Working around the ball, ★ sc in first sc, dec over next 2 sc. Rep from ★ around (12 sc).

Rnd 15: Dec 6 sc spaced evenly around (6 sc). Fasten off.

Basket

With size 00 hook and color B yarn, start at the bottom of the basket and ch 2.

Rnd 1: Make 6 sc in the 2nd ch from hook. *Do not join rnds.* Carry a piece of contrasting color yarn between the first and last sc to mark the beginning of the rnds.

Rnd 2: Inc in each sc around (12 sc)

Rnd 3: ★ Sc in first sc, inc in next sc. Rep from ★ around (18 sc).

Rnd 4: ★ Sc in first 2 sc, inc in next sc. Rep from ★ around (24 sc).

Rnd 5: (Work in *back loops only*) sc in each sc around (24 sc).

Rnds 6 through 10: Work even on 24 sc. Fasten off at end of Rnd 10.

To Finish

1. Cut 4 pieces of ribbon, each 4 inches long. Evenly space and glue or pin one end of each length of ribbon to the balloon at its widest diameter (see Balloon Ornament diagram, page 177).

2. Evenly space and glue or sew the other end of each piece of ribbon around the rim of the basket.

3. Use the pins to attach the sequins all over the balloon.

4. Run the length of gold cord through the top of the balloon and tie a loop for hanging.

5. Place small figures or a tiny gift in the basket and hang on the tree.

Snowball Fun

A boy and girl dressed in bright red and green snowsuits have fun tossing snowballs. They can hang from the tree as ornaments or be used to create a winter wonderland scene on a table or mantel. They also make great stocking stuffers.

MATERIALS

4-ply yarn: 1 oz. white, ½ oz. each of red and green, small amount of yellow
Small amount of stuffing
2 wooden beads, ¾ inch diameter, with painted faces and predrilled hole in one end (available in craft stores)

2 pipe cleaners, each 4 inches long
2 pipe cleaners, each 7 inches long
Yarn needle
White craft glue
Cord or satin ribbon for hanging
Crochet hook: G/6 (4.5 mm)

DIRECTIONS

To make the body form, fold the 7-inch pipe cleaner in half and push the folded end through the hole in the wooden bead head. Twist the 4-inch pipe cleaner once around the folded pipe cleaner ½ inch below the bead to form the arms. Repeat for the second ornament.

Snowsuit

Use red yarn for one ornament and green for the other.

PANTS: Beginning with the leg, chain 5.
Row 1: Single crochet in 2nd ch from hook and each ch across. Ch 1 to turn each row.
Rows 2 through 5: Sc in each stitch. Cut yarn at the end of Row 5. Make a second leg in the same way, but do not cut yarn.
Row 6: Sc in each sc, sc in each st of first leg.
Row 7: Sc in each st. Cut yarn. Sew leg seams.

Snowball Fun

JACKET BACK: Cut a 9-inch piece of yarn and set aside for later use. Ch 5.
Row 1: Sc in 2nd ch from hook and each ch across. Ch 1 and turn. Drop loop from hook; with 9-inch yarn ch 2, join by pulling dropped lp through lp on hook, sc in each of next 4 sc, ch 3 and turn.
Row 2: Sc in 2nd ch from hook and next ch, sc in each of next 4 sc, sc in each remaining ch. Ch 1 and turn.
Row 3: Sc in each st. Cut yarn.

JACKET FRONT (Make 2)
Ch 4.
Row 1: Sc in 2nd ch from hook and each of next 2 ch, ch 3 and turn.
Row 2: Sc in 2nd ch from hook and next ch, sc in each sc. Ch 1, turn.
Row 3: Sc in each st. Fasten off.
Sew the shoulder, side, and underarm seams. Slip the pipe-cleaner figure into the pants top and pants. Sew front seam of top and pants. Sew bottom of jacket to top of pants.

Boots (Make 2)

Using green yarn for one ornament and red for the other, ch 6.
Row 1: Sc in 2nd ch from hook and each ch across. Ch 1 to turn each row.
Row 2: Sc in each st.
Row 3: Sc, increasing 1 st in first and last sts.
Row 4: Sc in each st. Cut yarn. Sew front and bottom seams. Slip boots onto bottom of snowsuit legs.

Mittens

Using green yarn for one ornament and red for the second, ch 4.
Row 1: 6 sc in 2nd ch from hook.
Rnd 2: Sc in each st. Cut yarn. Slip on end of the pipe-cleaner arms and stitch to the end of each sleeve.

Hat/Scarf

Using green, ch 4.
Row 1: Sc in the 2nd ch from the hook and each of the next 2 chs. Ch 1 to turn each row.
Rows 2 through 8: Sc in each st. Ch 15 at end of Row 8. Cut yarn. Join yarn on opposite end, ch 15, cut yarn. To sew back seam, fold the piece in half and stitch opening closed. Cut a few strands of yellow yarn to desired length for the hair. Glue the yarn to the top of the bead head. Glue the hat to the head. You can give both figures a hat or make the second one with earmuffs.

Earmuffs

Using red yarn, ch 2.
Row 1: 2 sc in the 2nd ch from the hook, ch 5, 2 sc in 2nd ch from the hook. Cut yarn.
Glue a few strands of yellow yarn to the head as for the first ornament and glue earmuffs in place. With red yarn, ch 15 for scarf and tie around neck.

Large Snowball

Using white yarn, ch 2.
Rnd 1: 6 sc in the 2nd ch from the hook.
Rnd 2: 2 sc in each st.
Rnd 3: (Sc in next sc, 2 sc in next sc) 6 times.
Rnds 4 through 7: Sc in each st.
Rnd 8: (Sc in each sc, sc next 2 sc together) 6 times. Stuff with filling.
Rnd 9: (Sc 2 tog) 3 times. Cut yarn. Sew between hands so that the figure is holding the big snowball.

Small Snowball

Using white yarn, ch 2.
Rnd 1: 3 sc in 2nd ch from hook.
Rnd 2: 2 sc in each st.
Rnd 3: (Sc in next sc, 2 sc in next sc) 3 times
Rnd 4: Sc in each st.
Rnd 5: (Sc in next sc, sc next 2 sc tog) 3 times. Stuff with a small amount of filling.
Rnd 6: (Sc 2 tog) 3 times. Cut yarn. Sew to one hand of the second ornament figure.

To Finish

Make a 3-inch loop of cord or satin ribbon and attach to each one for hanging.

Candle Ornament

It's easy and inexpensive to fill the tree with candle ornaments made from scraps of yarn. The "flame" on each candle is created with yellow pipe cleaners that extend up through the crocheted sleeve.

MATERIALS

4-ply yarn: small amounts of red and white
12-inch yellow pipe cleaner

Beaded ornament trim (optional)
Crochet hook: F/5 (4 mm)

DIRECTIONS

Candle

Using red yarn, chain 12.

Row 1: Single crochet in the 2nd ch from the hook and each ch across. Ch 1 to turn each row.

Rows 2 through 4: Sc in each stitch. Cut yarn at the end of Row 4. Fold the pipe cleaner in half. Wrap the crocheted piece around the pipe cleaner with the folded end extending ½ inch above the red crocheted sleeve. Slipstitch seam from the top to the bottom.

Candle Holder

Using white yarn, ch 4. Join into ring. Ch 1.

Rnd 1: 12 sc in ring. Join.

Rnd 2: Ch 1, 2 sc in each st. Join.

RUFFLE

Ch 1, sc in next st, (★ ch 3, sc in same st 3 times more, ch 3, sc in next st ★). Repeat between ★s in each st around. Join and cut yarn.

To Finish

Push the 2 free ends of the pipe cleaner through the center of the holder. Pull them until the candle rests against the holder. Twist the extended pipe cleaner pieces under the ruffled holder and use them to secure the ornament to the tree branch.

Glue or stitch a green and red bead to the ruffled holder to look like a little holly decoration if desired. Or you might add some glitter all around the holder.

Candle Ornament

Reindeer in Santa's Boot

182

Reindeer in Santa's Boot

Rudolph the Red-Nosed Reindeer is tucked into Santa's boot for an unusual tree ornament. You can make this as one project or make the reindeer separately. The boot is made of black yarn, but you might want to use a bright Christmas red or green.

MATERIALS

4-ply knitting worsted yarn: small amounts black, brown, and red
10-inch brown pipe cleaner
Small amount of stuffing

Yarn needle
Silver cord for hanging
Crochet hook: G/6 (4.5 mm)

DIRECTIONS

Boot

With black yarn, chain 10.

Rnd 1: Single crochet in the 2nd ch from the hook and each of next 6 chs, half double crochet in next stitch, 4 double crochet in next st, hdc in next st, sc in each of next 6 ch on opposite side of original ch. *Do not join rounds.* Carry a piece of contrasting color yarn between the first and last sts to mark the beginning of the rnds.

Rnd 2: 2 sc in each of next 2 sc, sc in each of next 6 sc, 2 sc in each of next 6 sc, sc in each of next 6 sc, 2 sc in next sc.

Rnd 3: 2 sc in each of next 2 sc, sc in each of next 10 sc, 2 sc in each of next 6 sc, sc in each of next 10 sc, 2 sc in next sc.

Rnd 4: (Work in *back loops only* of this round.) Sc in each st.

Rnd 5: Sc in each st.

Rnd 6: Sc in each of next 16 sc, (sc next 2 sc together) 2 times, sc in next sc, (sc next 2 sc tog) 2 times, sc in each of next 13 sc.

Rnd 7: Sc in each of next 4 sc, (sc next 2 sc tog) 2 times, sc in next sc, (sc next 2 sc tog) 2 times, 2 sc in each of next 11 sc.

Rnd 8: Sc in each st. Join. Cut yarn. Fold the piece in half from front to back. Skip center front 3 sts, join yarn in next st with sc, mark st with piece of contrasting color yarn, sc in each of next 26 sc, mark last st with piece of contrasting color yarn. Ch 1 to turn each row.

Rnd 9: Sc, increase 1 st in first and last sts.

Rnd 10: Sc in each st. Cut yarn.

TONGUE

Join yarn with sc in first marked st.

Row 1: Sc in each of the 3 skipped sts, sc in last marked st. Ch 1 to turn each row.

Row 2: Sc, inc 1 st in first and last sts.

Rows 3 through 5: Sc in each st.

Row 6: Hdc in next st, dc in each of the next 2 sts, 2 triple crochet in next st, dc in each of next 2 sts, hdc in next st. Cut yarn.

LACES

Ch 75. Cut yarn. Lace boot.

Join yarn in skipped front lp of Rnd 4, sc in each st. Join. Cut yarn.

Reindeer

Using brown yarn, ch 2.

Rnd 1: 6 sc in 2nd ch from hook.

Rnd 2: 2 sc in each st.

Rnd 3: (Sc in next st, 2 sc in next st) 6 times.

Rnds 4 through 8: Sc in each st.

Rnd 9: (Sc in next sc, sc next 2 sc tog) 6 times. Stuff.

Rnd 10: (Sc 2 sc tog) 6 times.

Rnd 11: Sc in each st.

Rnd 12: 2 sc in each st. Join. Cut yarn.

NOSE

With red yarn, chain 2.

Rnd 1: 4 sc in the 2nd ch from the hook, join. Cut yarn. Join brown yarn and sc in each st.

Rnd 2: 2 sc in each st. Join. Cut yarn. Stuff.

Sew the head between Rnds 6 and 9.

EARS

Join yarn bet Rnds 3 and 4, ch 3, dc in same st, ch 3, join in same st. Cut yarn. Repeat for 2nd ear.

Fold the pipe cleaner in half for the antlers. Twist the ends to look like antlers. Attach to the top of the head between the ears.

To Finish

Using black yarn, make a French knot (see page 11) for each eye. Fill the boot with stuffing and place the reindeer's head on top of the boot opening. He will appear to be peeking out of the boot. Attach a cord through the back of the reindeer's head and the back top edge of the boot. Knot and hang.

Little Drummer Boy

This ornament measures 5 inches high and the drum is 3 inches in diameter. It can also be used as a centerpiece or with some of the other figures in a winter scene.

MATERIALS

4-ply knitting worsted yarn: small amounts of red, black, white, and yellow (or colors of your choice)

Stuffing

¾-inch diameter wooden bead with painted face and predrilled hole in one end (available in craft stores)

1 pipe cleaner (any color), 7 inches long

2 yellow pipe cleaners, each 5 inches long

Yarn needle

White craft glue

Crochet hook: F/5 (4 mm)

DIRECTIONS

To make the body form, fold the 7-inch pipe cleaner in half and push the folded end through the predrilled hole in the bead head. Twist the 5-inch pipe cleaner around the folded pipe cleaner ½ inch below the bead to form the arms.

Pants

Using black yarn, begin the pant leg with a chain 4.

Row 1: Single crochet in 2nd ch from the hook and each ch across. Ch 1 to turn each row.

Row 2: Sc in each stitch.

Row 3: Sc, increasing in first and last st.

Rows 4 through 8: Sc in each st.

Row 9: Sc in each of the next 4 sc; sc, half double crochet, double crochet, hdc, sc in next st (boot); sc in last st. Cut yarn.

Sew inseam from the first increase row to the bottom. Sew the bottom seam to form the boot.

SECOND PANT LEG

Work same as for first pant leg through Row 8.

Row 9: Sc in first st; sc, hdc, dc, hdc, sc in next st (boot); sc in each of last 4 sc. Cut yarn and finish as you did for the first pant leg.

Slip pants over the pipe-cleaner legs of the figure. Sew the front and back seam of the pants. To make a stripe on each pant leg, run red yarn down 1 inch of each side of pant legs. Secure inside the pants.

Jacket (Make 2)

Using red yarn, ch 7.

Row 1: Sc in the 2nd ch from hook and each ch across. Ch 1 to turn each row.

Rows 2 and 3: Sc in each st.

Row 4: (Sleeve): Sc in each st. Ch 5.

Row 5: (Sleeve): Hdc in the 2nd ch from hook and each of the next 3 ch, sc in each of next 6 sts, ch 5.

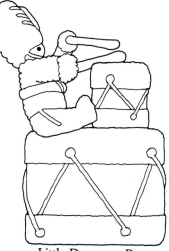

Little Drummer Boy

185

Row 6: Repeat Row 5. Ch 1 and turn.
Row 7: Sc first 2 sts together as one, sc in each of next 2 sts, sc last 2 sts tog as one. Cut yarn.

Gloves

Join the white yarn at the end of one sleeve, sc, hdc, sc all in the same st. Cut yarn. Rep from second sleeve. Sew seams, slip onto figure. Add ½-inch strip of yellow yarn to make a bar on the top of each shoulder.

Belt

Using black yarn, ch 18. Cut the yarn. Secure the belt around the doll's waist. Using yellow yarn and running stitch (see page 11), outline a buckle in the front center of the belt.

Hat

Using black yarn, ch 11.
Row 1: Sc in 2nd ch from hook and each ch across. Ch 1 to turn each row.
Rows 2 through 5: Sc in each st.
Row 6: Sc first 3 sts tog as 1, sc in next st, sc next 2 sts tog as 1, sc in next st, sc last 3 sts tog as 1. Cut yarn.
Using yellow yarn and running stitch (see page 11), embroider a feather emblem on the front of the hat. Sew back seam and glue hat to bead head.

CHIN STRAP
Run black yarn from side to side under the chin 2 times. Secure on each side of hat.

Large Drums

TOP AND BOTTOM (Make 2)
Using yellow yarn, ch 2.
Rnd 1: 6 sc in 2nd ch from hook. Join and ch 1.
Rnd 2: (Mark beginning of each rnd with colored yarn.) 2 sc in each st. Join. Ch 1.
Rnd 3: (Sc in next sc, 2 sc in next sc) 6 times. Join. Ch 1.
Rnd 4: (Sc in each of next 2 sc, 2 sc in next sc) 6 times. Join. Ch 1.
Rnd 5: (Sc in each of next 3 sc, 2 sc in next sc) 6 times. Join. Ch 1.
Rnd 6: (Sc in each of next 4 sts, 2 sc in next sc) 6 times. Join. Ch 1.
Rnd 7: (Sc in each of the next 5 sc, 2 sc in next sc) 6 times. Join. Cut yarn.

SIDES
Using white yarn, ch 10.
Row 1: Sc in 2nd ch from hook and each ch across. Ch 1 to turn each row.
Rows 2 through 43: Sc in each st. Cut yarn at end of Row 43. Sew short ends tog forming a tube. Sew the bottom in one end of the tube *through back sts only.*

BAND

Join yellow yarn in front lps on the circle, work 1 sc in each st around. Join. Ch 1.

Rnd 2: (Work *back lps only.*) Sc in each st. Join. Ch 1.

Rnd 3: Sc in each st. Join. Cut yarn.

Fold the band down and tack all around. Stuff until full.

Next, sew the top circle in position. Make the band in the same way as for the first band.

To Finish

Using the black yarn, make 4 French knots (see page 11), spaced evenly around each band. Run black yarn, on the diagonal, from French knot to French knot on the top and bottom of the drum as shown.

Small Drum

TOP AND BOTTOM

Using white yarn, ch 2.

Rnd 1: 6 sc in each st. Join. Cut yarn.

Rnd 2: 2 sc in each st. Join. Cut yarn.

SIDES

Using yellow yarn, ch 7.

Row 1: Sc in 2nd ch from hook and each ch across. Ch 1 to turn each row.

Rows 2 through 15: Sc in each st. Cut yarn at end of Row 15. Sew the short ends tog to form a tube. Sew the bottom piece in the tube.

BAND (Make 2)

Using white yarn, ch 21.

Row 1: Sc in 2nd ch from hook and each ch across. Cut yarn. Sew one band around the top and one around the bottom. Stuff until full. Sew the top in position.

To Finish

Using black yarn, make 4 French knots (see page 11) spaced evenly around each band. Run black yarn diagonally from French knot to French knot from top to bottom as shown.

Drum Sticks

Cut the remaining pipe cleaner in half. Stitch to each hand of the figure.

To Assemble

Attach the small drum to the larger drum. Stitch the figure to the drum so he is in a sitting position with the drumsticks on top of the little drum as shown in the drawing.

Filled with Romance

Cornucopias are romantic looking when made from silver and gold paper and trimmed with ribbons, lace, floral stickers, and braid. Each has an attached gold cord or ribbon for hanging and can be filled with small candies, gifts, sachets, or dried flowers such as baby's breath. The pattern is provided full size so you can trace it and make several from different colored papers. The little gift tins are made from cough drop containers, covered with gift wrapping or Contact paper and floral stickers.

MATERIALS

Sheet of Bristol board (available in art stores)
Sheet of shiny wrapping paper in gold, silver, and red or desired colors
Scraps of lace, ribbon, braid, and eyelet
Sticker stars, floral decals, etc.
Tracing paper
Rubber cement
White craft glue

DIRECTIONS

1. Apply rubber cement to the back of shiny paper and set aside to dry.
2. Apply rubber cement to one side of the Bristol board and set aside to dry.
3. Carefully mount the shiny paper to the Bristol board.
4. Trace the cornucopia pattern and transfer to the back of the Bristol board (see page 8).
5. Cut out the pattern.
6. Using a butter knife and a straight edge, score along the lines where indicated on the pattern.
7. Fold the flap to the inside and glue in position.

To Finish

1. Glue trim around edges. Glue raw edge of lace or eyelet trim around inside edge of cornucopia.
2. Decorate with stickers and decals on each side.
3. Add a hanging loop made from gold cord or ribbon.
4. Fill with desired treats and hang on the tree.
A gift idea: Fill little squares of bridal lace with potpourri and tie with a pretty ribbon. Place a sachet in each cornucopia and arrange in a pretty fabric-lined basket.

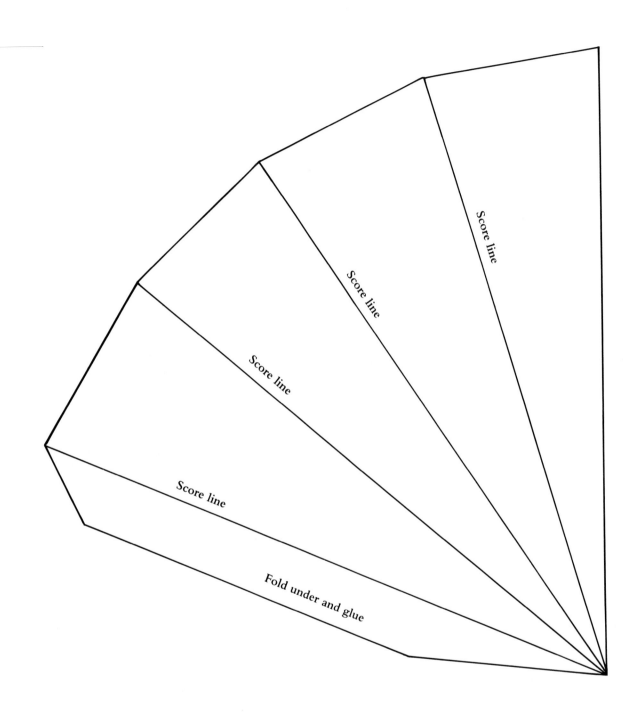

Score line

Score line

Score line

Score line

Fold under and glue

Index